Lorenzo Burge

Origin and Formation of the Hebrew Scriptures

Lorenzo Burge

Origin and Formation of the Hebrew Scriptures

ISBN/EAN: 9783337317324

Printed in Europe, USA, Canada, Australia, Japan

Cover: Foto ©ninafisch / pixelio.de

More available books at **www.hansebooks.com**

BY THE SAME AUTHOR

PRE-GLACIAL MAN and the ARYAN RACE $1.50

ARYAS, SEMITES AND JEWS,
      JEHOVAH AND THE CHRIST $1.50

LEE AND SHEPARD PUBLISHERS BOSTON

ORIGIN AND FORMATION OF THE

HEBREW SCRIPTURES

..... RECITING WHEN, WHERE, UNDER WHAT CIRCUMSTANCES, FOR WHAT PURPOSE AND BY WHOM THEY WERE WRITTEN, AS OBTAINED FROM THE WRITINGS OF THAT EMINENT PERSIAN NOBLEMAN AND HISTORIAN NEHEMIAH WHO WAS APPOINTED GOVERNOR OF PALESTINE B.C. 445. . . . WITH AN APPENDIX CONTAINING PROPHECY SUSTAINED IN THE HISTORIES OF EGYPT, ASSYRIA AND BABYLON; AND A REVIEW OF RADICAL VIEWS OF THE BIBLE ....

By LORENZO BURGE

AUTHOR OF "PRE-GLACIAL MAN AND THE ARYAN RACE" AND "ARYAS, SEMITES AND JEWS: JEHOVAH AND THE CHRIST"

PUBLISHED A.D. MDCCCXC

BY LEE AND SHEPARD 10 MILK STREET BOSTON NEXT "THE OLD SOUTH MEETING-HOUSE" AND CAN BE HAD OF ALL RESPECTABLE BOOK-DEALERS OR SAID BOOK WILL BE SENT BY MAIL UPON RECEIPT OF THE PRICE $1.00 ...

PREFACE.

THE Hebrew Scriptures are composed of all the books of the Old Testament except the Psalms, Proverbs, Ecclesiastes, and Song of Solomon. This collection was known to the Jews as the "Law and the Prophets," and is the foundation of our Bible.

Believers in the old theology claim that this collection, relating events thousands of years apart, was written by men especially inspired by the Deity for the work; that these men were mere instruments in his hands to record his will; and the verbal inspiration of the Bible as a whole is insisted on, and all unbelievers in this doctrine are by them denounced as infidels.

Later writers have taken an opposite position; they scout the idea of inspiration, deny the unity of the Bible, and proclaim it to be a manufacture from beginning to end, its writers having for personal ends formed from old legends and sun myths the remarkable history of the Hebrews recorded in the Old Testament, while the writers of the New Testament books were led by personal hate and spite to falsify the traditions of Jesus of Nazareth, called the Christ, and present to the world this false though wonderful record of his life and acts. These two extreme views are examined in the index.

Any person of common ability, desirous of ascertaining the authorship of the Hebrew Scriptures or the Old Testament, will notice that, with slight exceptions, it is written in the third person; that, like any other history, the author relates in his own words the events which happened at certain previous periods of time, and he quotes freely incidents and conversations *verbatim*. In the Mosaic history, he introduces his quotations with, "thus saith the Lord," "then answered Moses," "Moses said unto the people," etc. The whole tenor of the writing shows that Moses could not have written four of the books of the "Pentateuch," but that some other person did write it. The fifth book, Deuteronomy, is from the pen of Moses, translated by the author, *verbatim*, with a few notes and necessary explanations. The author, like Bancroft or any other historian, used the authorities at his command, making comments and explanations as he proceeded.

It is strange that, with all the critical examinations of the Scriptures made by German scholars, the peculiarities of the writer of the "Law and the Prophets" should not have been noticed. More especially as, when once pointed out, they are so pronounced as to be readily observed by the most careless reader. They run through the Old Testament to, and include, Nehemiah, also in portions of Isaiah and Jeremiah; and the same author writes the introductory passages of each of the other prophets.

In ancient times, books were written on skins of animals prepared for the purpose, attached together, and made into one continuous roll, as large as could be conveniently handled, or the roll was confined to one subject. When finished, the subject treated upon was marked on the roll. There were no punctuation or quotation marks, no chapter or verse. There were no separate pages, consequently no notes at the foot of the page, as is now done. All notes, comments, references, or explanations were made in the body of the writing.

In the Old Testament, the subject treated on was marked on the outside of the roll; and we have a roll marked Genesis, meaning the beginnings of things. The exode of the Hebrews is marked Exodus; the Levitical laws are recorded in the roll marked Leviticus; and the condition and numbering of the Israelites is in the roll marked Numbers, and so on. All the books of the Old Testament received their title from the principal subjects mentioned in the book or roll.

In this book we have given a slight sketch of the contents of each book or roll, with the purpose of calling the reader's attention to the main object of the author in writing or translating the work, which was to enforce on the notice of the new nation of Jews the lessons of faith in, and dependence on, Jehovah, their tutelary god. In the history, he constantly brings forward the fact that, when the Hebrews were loyal to their God, they were blessed with peace, prosperity, and length of days, and whenever they turned from their allegiance, and worshipped other gods, they were punished by wars, pestilence, famine, captivity.

PERSONAL.

WHILE I have been charged by critics who sustain the mediæval doctrines of the dark ages, with falsifying the Bible in my first book,[1] I have been censured by liberal Christian critics for ignoring, in my second volume,[2] the results of modern Biblical criticism, and for sustaining the truth of the Scriptures and the fact of and the necessity of miracles.

In answer to the charges of the first-named critics, I assert that, instead of falsifying the Bible, I have increased and enlarged it.

In that volume I revealed, hidden in the allegory in Genesis, a record of the evolution of, and the changes in the configuration of, the earth, and the creation of life, the laws governing the advance and retreat of the glacial period, and their effect in forcing man to "replenish the earth," during a period of thirty thousand years, with a history of the intellectual, moral, and spiritual advance of the Aryas for a period of ten thousand years, and their final deca-

---

[1] Pre-glacial Man and the Aryan Race.
[2] Aryas, Semites and Jews.

dence and fall, — the only history of that period yet known to man.

In answer to the second-named critics, I ignored the (so-called) scientific criticism of the Bible because I did not believe in it; and the present volume will show why I did not accept it.

In *this* volume will be found a history of the origin and formation of the Hebrew Scriptures, taken wholly from its pages, yet, until now, unknown. In this and the previous volumes, I have enlarged, not falsified, the Bible; I have sustained the fact and necessity of miracles, and in the present volume have proved the truths of prophecy by showing their strict fulfilment after hundreds of years had passed, or their continued life and action unto the present day.

LORENZO BURGE.

CONTENTS.

	PAGE
THE LAW.	15
BOOK OF BEGINNINGS	22
ORIGIN OF THE HEBREW RACE AND NATION	24
GENESIS	24
EXODUS	25
LEVITICUS	26
NUMBERS	26
DEUTERONOMY	27
JOSHUA.	27
JUDGES.	28
RUTH	30
SAMUEL	30
KINGS	31
CHRONICLES.	33
END OF THE HEBREW NATIONALITY	35
EZRA	35
NEHEMIAH	36
THE BEGINNING OF THE JEWISH NATIONALITY	36
THAT NEHEMIAH WROTE THE HEBREW SCRIPTURES, PROVED	48
ESTHER.	49
JOB	50

14 CONTENTS.

                                                            PAGE

NOT A PORTION OF THE LAW AND THE PROPHETS 51
    PSALMS 52
    PROVERBS AND ECCLESIASTES 54
    SOLOMON'S SONG 55

THE PROPHETS 55
    ISAIAH 55
    JONAH 57
    JEREMIAH 60
    EZEKIEL 66
    DANIEL 66
    ISAIAH THE YOUNGER 67

APPENDIX 73
    PROPHECY SUSTAINED 73
    EGYPT 74
    FULFILLED BY ASSUR-BANIPAL, KING OF ASSYRIA, B.C. 668 74
    FULFILLED BY NEBUCHADNEZZAR, KING OF BABYLON, B.C. 572 76
    FULFILLED BY CAMBYSES, THE KING OF PERSIA, B.C. 525 77
    ASSYRIA 80
    BABYLON 87
    RADICAL VIEWS OF THE BIBLE 104
    SCIENTIFIC CRITICISM 105
    VERBAL INSPIRATION 123

ORIGIN AND FORMATION OF THE HEBREW SCRIPTURES.

THE LAW.

A CAREFUL examination of the Old Testament shows that the most important part of the book is the work of one person. Who that person was we shall see later.

The main portion, including a part of Genesis to Esther, is a history of the covenants made by the Deity with Abraham, Isaac, and Jacob as a personal or household god; the national covenant or contract made by the Deity as Jehovah with the Hebrews, and the laws connected with and consequent thereon; the incidents leading thereto from the call of Abram to the completion of the work through Moses; and the results of the contract as shown in their history.

"The Book of the Law of Jehovah" is the nucleus of the Hebrew Scriptures, the cause of its being, and the means of its preservation.

This history is written in a free and flowing style with certain peculiarities of diction and expression which give internal evidence of the complete unity of the whole. It covers the whole life of the Hebrew nation to the captivity, records the return from captivity, the rebuilding of the temple at Jerusalem, the re-establishment of the worship of Jehovah, the formation of the Jewish nation, and its history to and including Nehemiah, and could not have been the work of any one previous to his time.

To fully appreciate the work, we must understand the circumstances under which it was written.

B.C. 606. Nebuchadnezzar conquered Judah and carried the king, Jehoiachim, with many of the inhabitants, into captivity. A year after, his son Jehoiachin, with many others, was also carried a captive to Babylon; and Zedekiah was placed as a tributary king on the throne. At this time, Jeremiah, who had foretold the captivity, prophesied that their captivity would be long; he wrote to those who had been carried into Babylon, "Build ye houses and dwell in them, and plant gardens and eat the fruit of them, take ye wives and beget sons and daughters, and take wives for your sons, and give your daughters to husbands, that they may bear sons and daughters, that ye may be increased there and not diminished; and seek the peace of the city whither I have caused you to be carried away captives, and pray unto the Lord for it; for in the peace thereof shall ye have peace." Seventy years, he says, they shall serve Babylon, then they shall return and rebuild the temple. Desolation, he says, shall reign in Judah, and Jerusalem shall become a heap.

Eighteen years after, B.C. 588, Nebuchadnezzar again proceeded against Jerusalem, took it, destroyed its walls, burned the temple, the palaces and houses to the ground, put out the eyes of the king, and carried him and the people captive to Babylon, thus ending the Hebrew nationality.

B.C. 536. When the Jews, who by permission of Cyrus returned from Babylon to Jerusalem, arrived at the end of their long journey—just seventy years from the date (B.C. 606) of the conquering of Judah by Nebuchadnezzar — they found the country desolate, without inhabitants, overgrown in some portions with weeds, bushes, and brambles, and other portions covered with forests where wild animals lurked in the thickets.

Jerusalem itself was a heap of rubbish; wild vines and weeds covered with living green the débris of the city; the streets were obliterated and desolation reigned supreme. This was the scene which met the eyes of the Jews when they reached the site of the holy city, the city of their hope and expectations.

These emigrants, who now for the first time looked upon the city of David, were of the third and fourth generations of those who had been carried into captivity; they were of Babylonian birth, and spoke the Babylonian language, the Aramaic.[1] Few, but those of the priestly caste, had retained a knowledge of Hebrew, the language of their fathers; to the remainder it was a dead language.

The exigencies of the settlement of a new country, together with the hostility of the neighboring tribes and nations, materially interfered with the establishment of schools, and advance in knowledge was very slow. The colony brought by Ezra seventy-nine years later, B.C. 457, and the thousand families who in B.C. 445 came with Nehemiah, also spoke the Aramaic language. The Hebrew national records, and the Book of the Law, were all in the native Hebrew tongue, and the obligations of the contract and the requirements of the Law were alike unknown to the people in general.

[1] In "Fresh Light from the Ancient Monuments," Professor Sayce says, "In the latter days of the Assyrian Empire, Aramaic, the language of Aram, became the common language of trade and diplomacy, which every merchant and politician was supposed to learn, and in still later times succeeded in supplanting Assyrian in Assyria, and Babylonian as well as Hebrew in Palestine, until in its turn it was supplanted by Arabic."

Ezra, a studious and learned man, had no force of character. For ten years he had been high-priest, but he had done nothing to make the "Law" familiar to the people until the arrival of Nehemiah.[1]

On the occasion of rejoicing at the completion of the walls of Jerusalem, Ezra, standing where he could be seen, read aloud from the Law, and this was interpreted to the people by some of the priests and Levites. Apparently this was the first time that the Law had been interpreted to them.

Here was a people forming a new nation, desirous apparently of establishing that nation on the contracts made by Jehovah with their fathers, yet having a very slight knowledge of that contract or the laws and requirements or obligations connected therewith. The Law was written in Hebrew, to them an unknown tongue; how should they be made acquainted with its requirements?

In this new birth of the nation, it was necessary that the people should know their obligations under the contract with Jehovah, and their duties under the Law. With the stimulus of new hopes and the beginning of a new nation, the govern-

---

[1] Ezra had so little energy that when he sorrowed for the unlawful marriages of the Jews he did nothing, until he was urged by others, who promised to support and aid him in purifying the people.

ment must be re-established on the basis of the old covenant. Besides this, they were generally ignorant of their own national history and of the ancient geography of their country. In their captivity, the records of the Hebrew history and governments had been scattered, some of them lost, and, being in Hebrew, if at hand, would have been of little use to the people.

If this nation was to be established on the foundation of the worship of Jehovah, the circumstances were ripe for some one to write in the vernacular a history of the incidents and events leading to the covenant made with their fathers, giving them a copy of the Law, its obligations, its cursings and its blessings, with a succinct history of events to their own time. The want was felt; it was pressing, and the want found the man. Books were collected, and after years of preparation and toil "The Law and the Prophets" translated from the Hebrew into Aramaic substantially as we now have it was produced.

The author of this work shows some peculiarities of diction, which enable us to trace his writing throughout the work. The most prominent of these are the superfluous use of the word "now," and the phrase "it came to pass," in commencing paragraphs; and the redundant use of the conjunction "and." These mannerisms are prominent from Genesis to Esther, also in portions of Isaiah and Jeremiah. One of the New-Testament writers uses the same expressions, probably unconsciously influenced by his familiarity with the Old Testament. They are not found elsewhere except incidentally in the Bible.[1]

In accomplishing his purpose, the author necessarily gives a history of the nation itself. He writes in a free, easy, almost colloquial style, and, bearing in mind the people's ignorance of their national history and of the geography of the country, he frequently breaks the thread of his narrative to give the old or Canaanitish names of cities or towns, and the present names of old places; he makes explanations of old customs, and refers to the time when certain events took place or certain things were done. At intervals he brings in genealogies as claiming the particular attention of the Jews; for instance, he breaks into the allegory in Genesis, to give the genealogy of Noah; and in Exodus, sixth chapter, he interrupts the narrative to give the genealogy of Moses and Aaron; in short, he endeavors to make their history plain to the Jews of Palestine, for whose

[1] Any one keeping these peculiarities in mind, commencing with Genesis, second chapter, can trace the writer throughout the Old Testament, and he will be convinced that one person wrote the whole work to Esther, and other portions as we have mentioned.

particular benefit he was writing. None of the many works to which he refers as authority for the truth of his statements are now known to exist, and it is solely to his labors as a historian that we are indebted for our knowledge of the early history of the Jewish nation.

That the Hebrew Scriptures were transcribed from very full records is shown by the frequent quotations of conversations, addresses, songs, etc., introduced by the words, "and the Lord God said," "and Abraham said," "and Jacob said," "and the Lord spake unto Moses and said," "and Moses said unto them." "Then sang Moses and the children of Israel this song," "and Samuel said," and others throughout the book. All communications of importance are given in literal transcriptions or translations of the original text.

BOOK OF BEGINNINGS.

Known to the Jews at this time (about B.C. 436) was a remarkable book or manuscript of Aryan origin, "The Book of Beginnings." In the Pentateuch this book was placed before the commencement of the history of the Hebrew race and nation, because of the nature of its contents.

Without comment or introduction the author commences in a literal translation, giving "God" as the name of the Deity acting, as in the original text. "In the beginning God created the heaven and the earth." This literal translation is continued through the creative week. At the fourth verse of the second chapter, he continues the account in his own words, adding to the original "God," the name of "Jehovah" as the name of the distinctive God who had done this work.[1]

The author believed in many gods, but worshipped only Jehovah, and he is determined that he only shall have the credit of the creation of man. In so doing he antedated the time when that name was given unto Moses as the name of the national or tutelary God of the Hebrews. This "Jehovah" God is continued through the Adam and Eve portion to Cain, when the word "God" is dropped, the proper name "Jehovah" only being used. When translating literally in the further construction of the work to the time of Moses, the author uses "God," or "Almighty God," as in the original text. When telling the story in his own words, he gives "Jehovah" as the name of the Deity.

In the story of the Deluge there are two accounts which in some way have become badly mixed; the original can be traced by the name

---

[1] The prohibition, "Thou shalt not take the name of Jehovah thy God in vain," was observed so strictly that in their writings and conversations the Jews substituted for his proper name the words "the Lord," so that throughout the Hebrew Scriptures those words cover the proper name "Jehovah."

24   ORIGIN OF HEBREW SCRIPTURES.

"God" given to the Deity, which has been literally translated. In the other account, the days are increased from forty to over a year; the name Jehovah or Lord is given as that of the Deity; clean and unclean beasts, and the law of blood for blood, are introduced; the sons of Noah are numbered, and names are given to them; also, there has been added a chronology from Noah to Abraham. All of these changes and additions were made after the establishment of the Hebrew religion.

ORIGIN OF THE HEBREW RACE AND NATION. — GENESIS.

After completing the translation of "The Book of Beginnings," the author commences his history of the Hebrew race and nation. Beginning with Abram, he relates the incidents which caused him to leave Ur of the Chaldees, and finally migrate to the land of promise, giving his personal history and adventures; the promises made to and the agreements entered into by him, his change of name, and the purpose and meaning of the rite of circumcision; he records the main incidents in the lives of Isaac and Jacob, the events leading Jacob and his sons into Egypt, and the life of Joseph.[1]

[1] As Abram was native of a country full of public libraries, where every one could read and write, he undoubtedly kept a diary

The servitude of the Israelites is then shown; the infancy, and partially the life of Moses, to the time when he is selected by Jehovah as an agent to work out his purposes. All this, covering several hundred years, is evidently taken from full records, as is shown in the frequent quotations literally translated.

EXODUS.

The initial steps in the Exodus are minutely described; the conditional agreement between Jehovah and the Israelites; the results of that agreement in the release of the people from the bondage of Egypt, and the covenant or contract made between Jehovah and the Israelites, which is sealed by the blood from the altar. This contract, and the laws consequent thereon, are translated literally, with occasional explanatory notes, and with such connecting sentences and words as were necessary for a perfect understanding of the subject.

It may be well to notice that in the twentieth chapter, eleventh verse, the reason given for observ-

of his movements and actions. He would probably teach his son the same knowledge. It is apparently from such personal journals or records that the author obtained a knowledge of the personal incidents in the lives of the Patriarchs which he has related. In translating he gives the only names of the Deity known to the Patriarchs, "God" or "Almighty God." When using his own language, he adds the name Jehovah.

ing the Sabbath day is very different from the original, which we have from Moses himself in Deut. v. 15. "Remember that thou wast a servant in the land of Egypt, and that the Lord thy God brought thee out thence through a mighty hand and by a stretched-out arm; *therefore* the Lord thy God commanded thee to keep the Sabbath day." This statement is re-enforced in the twenty-third chapter of Exodus, "Six days thou shalt do thy work, and on the seventh day thou shalt rest; that thine ox and thine ass may rest, and the son of thy handmaid and the stranger may be refreshed."

In this book is also given an account of the setting-up of the Tabernacle, and the laws regulating the worship of Jehovah.

LEVITICUS.

In Leviticus these laws are continued, with laws relating to their future action, when they shall possess the promised land.

NUMBERS.

In Numbers these laws are continued and finished. The Israelites, fearing to enter the promised land, are detained in the wilderness forty years. The history of these forty years was apparently lost, as only a very meagre account is given of their life and journeyings. Previous to entering the promised land those over twenty years of age were numbered.

DEUTERONOMY.

The author makes this statement respecting Deuteronomy, " These be the words which Moses spake unto all Israel." This statement is verified in the contents of the book, which are written in the first person, with introductory remarks, and some notes and explanations by the author, such as giving in the fourth chapter a list of the cities of refuge on the east side of Jordan. In the sixth chapter he records the death of Aaron and the separation of the tribe of Levi, and in the last chapter he relates the incidents attending and records the death of Moses.

JOSHUA.

He follows the footsteps of Joshua, giving an account of the principal conflicts with the Canaanites, emphasizing the blessing of success following a faithful performance of their obligations to Jehovah, and the curse of defeat or death following disobedience.

In giving an account of the battle against the five kings before Gibeon, the author, immediately after his relation of the stupendous and long-continued hail-storm, during which "were more" (of the enemy) "that died with hail-stones than they whom the children of Israel slew with the sword," he suddenly breaks into the historical narrative, and, oblivious of the incongruity of the terrible hail-storm, and the shining of the sun and moon, he introduces a passage from the book of Jasher (supposed to have been a book of heroic poems), in which Joshua is represented as commanding the sun and moon to stand still: "Sun, stand thou still upon Gibeon, and thou, moon, in the valley of Ajalon." This poetic command was evidently believed in by the historian as an actual fact, for he adds, "The sun stood still, and the moon stayed, until the people had avenged themselves upon their enemies; and there was no day like that, before it or after it, that the Lord hearkened unto the voice of a man; for the Lord fought for Israel."[1]

After this digression, he again takes up the historical narrative of the battle, and finishes it.

JUDGES.

In the period of the Judges, after the settlement of the tribes in their various localities, and

---

[1] It was evidently the author's purpose, in making this quotation from Jasher, to bring prominently to the notice of the Jews, for their encouragement, the power of Jehovah, his particular care of his chosen people, and his prompt answer to the perfect trust shown by Joshua in his power and good-will.

the death of Joshua, there seems to have been a disintegration of the Hebrews. Each tribe pursued its own way, and made war or peace at pleasure. This disintegration gave opportunity for the neighboring nations to overcome and subdue them separately, and place them in bondage. There being no central government, no records were kept, and the author consequently had only startling and strange occurrences, or noble incidents and actions handed down by tradition, to record. It is not a connected history, but a series of striking events exemplifying the results of the law of blessing and cursing, which the author brings into prominent notice, as a warning to his people. The life of Samson is apparently given to show the application of the same law as applied to the individual. Samson was vowed or consecrated to Jehovah as a Nazarite; he was endowed by Jehovah with extraordinary strength; this power he retained as long as he was true to his vow; his uncut hair was the sign and symbol of his vow; when he allowed it to be cut he lost his power; afterward, having repented, and his hair, the sign of his vow, having grown again, at his earnest solicitation, Jehovah restores to him his strength, which he uses in the destruction of the Philistines.

The period of the Judges was apparently without law; there being no central government, each tribe did whatever it deemed best. The historian speaks of it as a time "before there was any king in Israel," when "each man did that which was right in his own eyes." In illustration of this want of law, and of their falling away from the worship of Jehovah and its results, he relates a series of events which took place in the early days of the Judges, some three hundred years before the date of Samson, when the setting-up and worship of strange gods by one of the tribes leads to deeds of violence, and finally to the death of some fifty thousand Israelites on the one side, and the destruction of twenty-five thousand men and the almost total wiping-out of the tribe of Benjamin on the other.

RUTH.

"Ruth" is a charming story of events taking place about two hundred years before Samson, illustrating the law of heredity, but introduced here apparently to show the result of faith in Jehovah, even by a Moabitess, and to give the genealogy of David.

SAMUEL.

"Samuel," in reality the first book of Kings, while in part a continuation of Judges, containing the personal histories of Eli and Samuel, is principally taken up with the events leading to the choice of Saul as king; his prowess, his impatience with the restraints of the law; the early history of David, his valor and discretion; the love of Jonathan and David, the adventures of David as an outlaw, and the death of Saul; the accession of David to the throne; his success in solidifying the nation, in subduing the surrounding nations, in establishing peace, and the great increase of the nation in power and wealth.

KINGS.

In Kings the history of David is continued; his resolve to erect a temple to Jehovah, for which he prepares the means; the placing of Solomon on the throne; the death of David; the erection of the Temple by Solomon, his glorious reign, the enlargement of the dominion, power, and wealth of Solomon, and his death are recorded.

The formation of the monarchy, and the reigns of Saul, David, and Solomon, are perhaps the most romantic as well as the most interesting portions of Hebrew history, to the events of which the Jew refers with pride and delight. While this portion is given in some detail, the history from Joshua down is made to emphasize the lesson he is desirous of teaching the Jews, namely, the constant fulfilment of the blessings and cursings of the law.

The histories of the divided kingdoms of Israel and Judah are then taken up and carried on side by side. The government of each of the kings, the character and result of their reigns in the light of their obligations to Jehovah, the good resulting from obedience and the ill effects of disobedience, are portrayed to the destruction of Samaria and the carrying of Israel captive to Assyria, B.C. 721. The reason given therefor is that the Israelites "did those things that were not right against the Lord their God." "So was Israel carried away out of their own land to Assyria unto this day."

The author interrupts his judgments of the reigns of Israel and Judah, to give his people a glimpse of the doings of the early prophets, the chief of whom at this time were Elijah and Elisha. These prophets prophesied only of the near future of the Hebrew nation. They had much to do with public events, and we consequently obtain more or less of the history of the two nations for some seventy or eighty years. These, with other prophets, held a conspicuous position among the Hebrews, and served to keep alive, by their teachings and their acts, the waning authority of Jehovah. About eighty years after the death of Elisha, in the reign of Uzziah, king of Judah, Isaiah appears as a prophet, and takes even a more conspicuous position in Judah than did the former prophets.

After the destruction of Israel the author continues the judgments of the kings of Judah, occasionally recording incidents of national importance or of religious interest.

In the reign of Josiah, the Temple was by his order cleaned and repaired; for seventy-five years it had been desecrated by the worship of other gods or had lain deserted. During this cleansing a copy of the "Book of the Law" was found and brought to Josiah, who re-established the worship of, and with the people renewed their covenant with, Jehovah.

CHRONICLES.

The early part of Chronicles contains genealogies from Adam to the captivity, taken from the "Books of the Kings of Israel and Judah."

The author then begins a separate history of Judah, commencing with the death of Saul and the choice of David as king. Passing over most of what had been written of David in the book of Samuel, he gives in some detail David's preparation for removing the ark of the covenant to, and its establishment in, Jerusalem, the appointing the services of worship, and the renewal of the covenant of their fathers.[1]

He then gives an account of the preparations made by David for the erection of the Temple, his making Solomon king, and of David's death.

Solomon built the Temple, placed therein the ark of the covenant, the altar, the molten sea, the lavers, candlesticks, table, and all the various instruments and utensils used in the worship of Jehovah, and dedicated the Temple with great pomp and rejoicing. He became very rich, many kings sent him presents, and others paid him tribute. He built Tadmor of the desert and other cities, and the country was very prosperous.

An account of the events in the reigns of the kings of Judah, much more full than that in Kings, is given, the reign of each king being again judged as having done "that which was right," or as having "done evil," in the sight of the Lord.

In the reign of Uzziah, king of Judah, Isaiah the prophet appears, and for the next fifty years, during the reigns of Uzziah, Jotham, Ahaz, and Hezekiah, he is a prominent figure in the history of Judah. Some eighty years after his death, in the reign of Josiah, Jeremiah appears, and, until

---

[1] This was the first national acknowledgment and renewal of the covenant made by their fathers with Jehovah since the days of Joshua.

the destruction of Jerusalem and the captivity of the people, he does not cease to warn and advise them.

END OF THE HEBREW NATIONALITY.

The book of Isaiah should be read in connection with the histories of the kings in whose reigns he lived, and that of Jeremiah should accompany the history of King Josiah and the other kings to the destruction and fall of Jerusalem. The stirring events of the last years of the Hebrew nation, which are mentioned in a few paragraphs in Chronicles, make a large part of the book of Jeremiah, and they give a vivid and lifelike picture of the closing scenes of the first or Hebrew nationality.

. . . . .

Seventy years after the taking of Jerusalem by Nebuchadnezzar, the returning Jews arrived at the site of the holy city. Here they laid the corner stone of a new Temple to be dedicated to the worship of Jehovah, the tutelar and national God of their fathers.

EZRA.

In Ezra we find the history of the movement, a list of those who returned from the captivity, and a sketch of what had been done until the coming of Nehemiah, ninety years after the first arrivals.

NEHEMIAH.

In Nehemiah we have a continuation of the history of the new nation in the first person, until he returned to Persia.

THE BEGINNING OF THE JEWISH NATIONALITY.

To Nehemiah is due the credit of rebuilding the walls of Jerusalem, restoring the ancient religion, and establishing on a firm basis the poor and struggling colony of Jews in Palestine, still weak and scattered and without national organization, after ninety years of growth as a Persian dependency.

Still greater honor belongs to him for his labors in collecting together the Hebrew records, scattered as they were throughout Persia and Babylonia; translating into the Aramaic tongue (the language of Babylonia) the contract made by their fathers with Jehovah, together with the law, and the blessings and cursings connected therewith; and also, from the records mentioned, translating into the same vernacular an epitome of the history of their people for a thousand years, with particular reference to the results of their contract with Jehovah as shown in each period of their existence; a work without which we should to-day have no Old Testament, and perhaps no Bible.

As the founder of the second or Jewish nationality, Nehemiah deserves a more prominent position than has been given him.

He was a man of eminence and wealth; a devout believer in Jehovah; a man of great energy and perseverance, and a trusted friend of the king of Persia.

Excited to compassion by the report of the poverty, suffering, and helpless condition of the colony of his faith in Palestine, and desirous of aiding and strengthening the infant nationality, he obtained leave of absence for a term of years from his sovereign, and with the appointment of governor, and with letters of credit to various rulers and other officials to aid him in his purpose of rebuilding the walls of Jerusalem and a palace for the governor's residence, he proceeded on his journey.

On arriving at Jerusalem, he made a private inspection of the city, and, finding it still "lying waste," he called together the priests, nobles, and rulers, and, rebuking them, proposed that they unite in building again the city walls. Stung by his rebuke, and aroused by his enthusiasm, they resolved to attempt the work. Each prominent family agreed to build a certain portion of the wall; thus apportioned, and urged by a spirit of emulation, the wall began to appear above the surrounding débris.

When it was about half built, the Samaritans, Ammonites, and others, enemies of the Jews, heard of it, and they "conspired together to come and to fight against Jerusalem and to hinder it." The people living in the neighborhood of these opposing nations also attempted to dissuade the Jews from continuing the work, saying "they will be upon you." Nothing daunted, however, Nehemiah armed the people, and set some to watch while others builded. He encouraged the nobles and rulers to continue, claiming that Jehovah would help and protect them. He also set his own servants, part to work on the walls, and part with weapons to watch. The builders and "every one had his sword girded to his side," and a watch was kept up day and night.

In the midst of these proceedings, trouble arose among the people. This building interrupted their work at home; some of them were in debt, and had mortgaged their farms; the children of others had become, or were liable to become, bondservants to their richer brethren.

Aroused to indignation by this state of affairs, Nehemiah called together the nobles, rulers, and wealthy men; reproved them for their greed, showing what had been done by the Jews in Babylonia and Persia for the relief of their poorer countrymen, and fairly shamed them into releasing their debtors, and restoring to their homes those who had become bond-servants.

In connection with this matter, Nehemiah says that former governors had received large sums from the people, as salaries; and that "even their servants bore rule over the people, but so did not I;" on the contrary, all his "servants worked upon the wall, and for twelve years he received no salary," supporting personally his whole establishment, and in addition he says, "there were daily at my table one hundred and fifty of the Jews and rulers, besides those that came unto us from among the heathen that are about us."

In the face of the threats of their foes, and the lukewarmness and even the secret opposition of some of the Jews, Nehemiah continued the work until the walls were up, the gates set in place, and the work finished. He then established rules with regard to the opening and shutting of the gates, and placed the city in charge of his brother, and the ruler of the palace. Thus far this history of Nehemiah is written in the first person, and is his own account of his individual work as governor. From this time he uses the public records in the continuation of his history, occasionally, however, injecting his distinct personality into the record.

The completion of this great work aroused the

people to a desire (perhaps aided by some judicious words of Nehemiah) for a knowledge of the law and of their obligations under it. They therefore assembled in the city and requested Ezra, the priest, to bring "the book of the law of Moses," and read it to them. This was done. Ezra read the Hebrew record, and, as he read, some of the Levites and scribes translated the sentences into the language of the people (the Aramaic), "and the ears of all the people were attentive unto the book of the law." And Nehemiah said unto the people, "this day is holy unto the Lord your God." He told them to be joyful and they rejoiced, "*because they had understood the words that were declared unto them.*" Notwithstanding Ezra had been with them ten years, this was apparently the first time that that generation had heard and understood the words of the law.

This did not satisfy them, for the next day they again came together, and again called upon Ezra and the scribes, "*even to understand the words of the law.*" As they read, it was found that that very week was the time for the Feast of the Tabernacles; and they were told to gather palm and other branches, and make booths on the roof tops and in the streets, and eat under them and rejoice; and they made booths, and sat under them, "and there was very great gladness. Also, *day by day, from the first day unto the last day*, he (Ezra) read in the book of the law of God."

Taking advantage of the new religious enthusiasm of the people, Nehemiah caused a written covenant to be drawn up, binding the signers of the covenant, under an oath and a curse, to "walk in God's law which was given by Moses," and "to observe and do all the commandments of the Lord our God," at the same time binding themselves to support the temple services, to bring their offerings of the first fruits of all their possessions, and to pay tithes for the support of the priesthood. This covenant was signed by Nehemiah, by the priests, Levites, and the rest of the people.

This matter, which was a work of time, — requiring not only perseverance, but also a persuasive ability to overcome objections and reconcile opposing interests, — having been accomplished, the next thing was to people the city.

It is worthy of note that in the ascription of praise with which this covenant begins, Jehovah is for the first time addressed as "Thou, even thou, art Lord alone; thou hast made heaven, the heaven of heavens, with all their host, the earth, and all things that are therein, the seas, and all that is therein; and thou preservest them all; and the host of heaven worshippeth thee."

The Jews generally had established themselves

in various towns and localities outside of Jerusalem, being engaged principally in farming and in the raising of sheep and cattle. Jerusalem remained almost uninhabited. It was the home of the governor and the seat of government, "and the rulers of the people dwelt at Jerusalem." Nehemiah gives a list of 3044 inhabitants.

A call being made for people to occupy the city, a few offered to do so, but the number was so small, it was decided that one in every ten of the inhabitants of Palestine should remove to Jerusalem, and who should go was determined by lot. The natural increase in Palestine, in ninety years of peace, would give at least a half-million of inhabitants, and this movement would give to Jerusalem fifty thousand citizens, and make it a city of some prominence and importance.

To carry out this programme, several years were necessary. Débris was cleared away, streets were laid out, houses built, and all the various trades and occupations necessary to the requirements of a large city were provided. This done, Jerusalem began to take upon itself an appearance worthy its old name and reputation.

All this work was done openly, with the full knowledge and sanction of the king of Persia, and in some points directed by him. Nehemiah says that "Pethahiah the son of Meshezabeel, of the children of Zerah the son of Judah, was at the king's hand in all matters concerning the people."

Finally, when the repeopling of the city had been accomplished, it was determined that the walls of the city should be dedicated. The city was now a city in fact as well as in name; the walls protected fifty thousand people, and there would now be a meaning in the service. We are given an account of the services, and of the enthusiasm of the people; "for God had made them rejoice with great joy; the wives also and the children rejoiced, so that the joy of Jerusalem was heard afar off."

To establish the services of the Temple on a firm basis, treasurers were appointed over "the chambers for the treasures, for the offerings, for the first fruits, and for the tithes; to gather into them out of the fields and the cities the portions of the law for the priests and Levites."

Nehemiah had been at Jerusalem apparently about ten years; on his arrival he had found the Jews dispirited and poor, without a religion, without a purpose; Palestine a mere colony, dependent on Persia, and Jerusalem a waste. By his great energy, skill, and perseverance, he had changed the whole aspect of affairs, and when he returned to Persia, in accordance with his original promise to the king, he left the country prosperous, full of enthusiasm for their new religion, and with a growing patriotism for their renewed nationality. During his absence he retained his rank as governor, and his establishment, with its freedom of support for the homeless and strangers arriving at Jerusalem.

He found the king at Babylon, and he employed his time, while in Babylonia and in Persia, in searching for and gathering together the various religious, biographical, and historical works mentioned by him as authorities for his history. The Jews, upon the destruction of their nation, had carried with them into Babylon the records of their national history; these were still in the hands of their descendants, and from them they were obtained by Nehemiah.

The author of the Maccabees says that "*Nehemiah gathered together the acts of the kings and the prophets, and of David, and the epistles of the kings concerning the holy city,*" and credits him with "*founding a library;*" he also speaks of "*the writings and commentaries of Nehemiah,*" and says of the library, and of other things collected by Judas, "They are still with us."

Twelve years from the date of his first visit to Jerusalem, Nehemiah obtained permission to return to the city of his adoption. On his arrival he resumed his duties as governor. He found some abuses had grown up in his absence which needed his personal attention, and he continues the narration of events in the first person.

In accordance with the requirements of the law, the Ammonites and Moabites had been "separated from Israel" and had been refused admission to the congregation. Eliashib the priest, however, was allied unto Tobiah the Ammonite, and, despite the action of the people, he had seized a great chamber, — "where aforetime they laid the meat offering, the frankincense, and the vessels and the tithes of the corn, the new wine, and the oil," — for the use of Tobiah, and no one had dared to interfere. As soon as known to Nehemiah, he proceeded at once to dispossess Tobiah. "I cast forth (he says) all the household stuff of Tobiah out of the chamber; then I commanded and they cleansed the chamber, and thither brought I again the vessels of the house of God, with the meat offering and the frankincense."

Owing to the neglect of the people to pay the tithes of the Levites, they had sought other means of support. For this he rebuked the rulers, and brought the Levites back to Jerusalem, "and all Judah paid the tithes of corn, wine, and oil," and he appointed treasurers to receive and disburse the same.

He found a general disregard for the Sabbath;

men attending to their work, merchants buying and selling as on other days. After some trouble he rectified this desecration. Learning that some of the Jews had married daughters of Ashdod, Ammon, and Moab, he caused them, as well as a grandson of Eliashib the high-priest, to leave the city, and thus cleansed it from all strangers.

Having by his energy and decision rid the city of backsliding Jews, cleansed the priesthood, and restored the proper worship of Jehovah, he commenced the great work which he had resolved upon, and for which he had prepared while in Babylonia and Persia.

In his first visit, Nehemiah had seen the necessity for making the people better acquainted with their obligations as the wards of Jehovah. Their quick backsliding from the position in which he left them a few years before emphasized this necessity, and at his first leisure he proceeded to translate for the use of the new nation the book of the law. But this was not all; he had several great objects to accomplish.

First, To give to the Jews a full and clear history of all the circumstances connected with the call of Abraham, and the beginning of their race, and of the principal events leading up to the covenant or contract made by Jehovah with their fathers.

Second, To make them acquainted with the contract itself, its blessings and cursings, and the laws connected therewith and consequent thereon.

Third, To give them, as far as possible, a knowledge of the historical events of importance, their localities, and such explanatory notes as would make the incidents of their ancient history familiar to them. And,

Fourth, To trace for their encouragement on the one hand, and their warning on the other, the results of the blessings and cursings of the law as exemplified in their individual and national histories. This thought, it will be seen, is carried out in every portion of the history he has written. If we read the story in this light, it will be found to be a perfect history of the dealings of the Deity as Jehovah with that people.

Every civilized nation on the earth had its god or gods who were the objects of worship, and who were credited by those nations with giving them peace, plenty, earthly prosperity, and success in war. This loyalty was required by Jehovah. Serving other gods was rebellion, disloyalty, treason, and was sternly punished by the general law of nations. In the case of the Hebrews it was more; it was a departure from the contract made by the fathers in the formation of the nation, a denial of their obligations to Jehovah and their dependence on him. In their constitution it merited severe punishment, and Nehemiah calls their particular attention to this matter in the judgments he gives of the rulers or judges of the Israelites, and of every reign of the kings of Israel and Judah.

These "writings and commentaries" of Nehemiah were ever after treasured by the Jews, and, with the prophetical works, became "the Law and the Prophets" of the Hebrew Scriptures of the time of the Christ.

THAT NEHEMIAH WROTE THE HEBREW SCRIPTURES, PROVED.

. . . . . .

There is no direct statement in the Bible that Nehemiah wrote the "Law and the Prophets;" but the circumstantial evidence is so strong as to make it morally certain that no one but he could have done it.

We think that we have proved in the preceding pages that the "Law and the Prophets" was the work of one hand.

It is certain that until his advent the Jews in Palestine were ignorant of the law of their fathers. They had even forgotten their feast days. It was through the influence of Nehemiah that the Jews renewed their compact with Jehovah. He organized and put in full operation the Temple services with the priests and Levites, and gathered the tithes for their support. He gave the new nation its material and religious start or impulse. He saw the people must have the law and its obligations in their own language, or it would again be forgotten. He it was who collected the necessary books forming a library of Hebrew, Historical, Personal, Epistolary, and other books, the names of twenty or thirty of which are mentioned or quoted as authorities. His interest in the well-being of the new nation and in establishing the worship of Jehovah on a firm basis was very strong, and he is the only person of sufficient energy and determination to accomplish such an undertaking, which would be a work of years. Tradition says he was governor for forty years, and lived to a good old age.

Finally, all commentators agree that the first six and the thirteenth chapters of the book of Nehemiah were written by him. An examination of these chapters shows the same peculiarities of style, the same mannerisms, as do all the other books of the "Law and the Prophets," and it is certain that if he wrote the chapters mentioned he must have written the whole work.

ESTHER.

In Esther we find recorded the events in the life of the Jews in Persia, which led to the establishment of the feast of Purim. Those events, taken, as the author says, from "the chronicles of the kings of Media and Persia," are evidently extracts from official documents. They are not of Jewish origin, as they contain no reference to the early history of the Hebrews, nor do they mention the name of Jehovah. In the simplicity of their statements they bear internal evidence of their truth. These events happened about one hundred years after the commencement of the captivity of the Jews, and give evidence of the great numbers and position of the Jews in Persia at that time. The author adds this to his history, apparently for two reasons. The first, because it showed the continued care of Jehovah in saving his people from slaughter; the second, that he might introduce the feast to the Jews in Palestine.

In order of time, "Daniel" precedes Esther, but, because of its prophetical utterances, it is placed with the other prophetical books. As a continuation of the history of the Jews, it should be read before Esther.

JOB.

The book of Job is evidently a Persian production. The scene of the poem is laid in Southern Babylonia, on the shore of the Persian Gulf. The character of the Deity as therein set forth is

Persian, not Mosaic. Satan was a being unknown to the Jews until after their Persian nationality had given them a knowledge of the Persian religion. The Mosaic or Jewish name of the Deity is used only by Nehemiah in his introduction, and in the answer of the Deity to Job, where he interpolates "Jehovah" as the name of the Deity speaking. In the conversations throughout, "God" and "the Almighty" are the names given to the Deity.

The book has nothing to do with either the religious or material history of the Jews, and the author's object in including this book, we think, is plain. He desired to enlarge the Jews' idea of Jehovah. This poem showed

First, God's special knowledge of each individual; all his children are known to and cared for by him.

Second, It controverted the Jewish idea that personal misfortune, sickness, or disease was proof of a vicious life, and

Third, It gave a more glorious and powerful picture of the Deity than any presented by Moses or the Prophets, and this picture, the author claimed, represented Jehovah.

NOT A PORTION OF THE LAW AND THE PROPHETS.

Between Job and the prophetical works are the PSALMS, PROVERBS, ECCLESIASTES, and SONG OF SOLOMON. None of these books have the slightest bearing on the purpose Nehemiah had at heart; they are no part of the material or religious history of the Hebrews. They have no introduction, nor is there any cause for their appearance in this place. David performed on the harp before the Lord, and it is possible some of the Mosaic Psalms may have been written by him, but most of them are far beyond his spiritual position and knowledge.

PSALMS.

Trinitarian commentators acknowledge that many of the Psalms are wrongly attributed to David. They generally divide them into five parts, as belonging to five periods of time, extending to the second nationality after the return from the captivity.

In 1 Chron. xvi., we have David's song of praise upon the establishment of the ark in Jerusalem. This song is thoroughly Mosaic, and gives us an utterance of David's, wherewith to try the Psalms. If we compare this production with the greater part of the Psalms, we find a world-wide difference. It is almost impossible that the same hand which penned that ascription of praise should have also written the 19th Psalm, "The heavens declare the glory of God;" the 23d, "The Lord is my shepherd;" the 24th, "The earth is the Lord's;" the 34th, "Trust in God;"

or the 30th, 39th, 40th, 42d, 43d, 51st, and many others.

It is true we have in 2 Sam. xxii. a song of praise of a higher character than that mentioned in 1 Chron. xvi.; but on examination we find it is not David's, and does not belong there. No occasion calls for it; it is pushed in without cause between the 21st and 23d chapters: it interrupts the narrative; we find further that it is a copy of the 18th Psalm, and the incidental reference to the Temple shows it was not written until after the death of David.

The 22d, 26th, 27th, 28th, and other Psalms ascribed to David also have allusions to the Temple. Others, like the 79th, 100th, and 137th, were evidently written while the Hebrews were in captivity. The 107th, 122d, 126th, 135th, 138th, 147th, and others refer to the rebuilding of Jerusalem after the return from captivity.

Many of the Psalms recognize God as the creator and sustainer of the universe, but no other Old Testament writers until Isaiah the younger, in the time of the captivity, do so.

In the 17th Psalm, and perhaps in one or two others, there is a distinct recognition of a future life.

David was a zealous supporter of the authority of Jehovah and of the Mosaic law throughout his life, and always acknowledged his dependence on

Jehovah for his success. In this, he was a man after God's own heart, but in this only. Judged by the light of his time, he was not only a successful but a good king. Yet he was an adulterer, a murderer, and a cruel and bloodthirsty conqueror. While he might have believed it was his duty to utterly destroy the enemies of his country, such acts as are described in 2 Sam. xii. 31, were not called for. "And he brought forth the people (the Ammonites) that were therein, and put them under saws, and under harrows of iron, and made them pass through the brick-kiln, and thus did he unto all the cities of the children of Ammon." That is, he sawed them asunder, tore them to pieces with the harrow, and baked them alive in the brick-kilns. Can such a foul murderer, such a cruel and bloody conqueror, have written the Psalms mentioned in the paragraphs above? Impossible. Some of the Mosaic Psalms may have been written by him, but those that are generally loved and indorsed by Christians are the work of a later period, a higher and more spiritual inspiration; they are a prevision of the coming of the Christ and of his teachings.

PROVERBS AND ECCLESIASTES.

Proverbs and Ecclesiastes are not religious writings; incidentally they show influences of a higher type than the time of Solomon.

SOLOMON'S SONG.

Commentators have in vain endeavored to find a meaning in Solomon's Song. If it is remembered that through the whole life of the Hebrew nation large numbers worshipped Ashtoreth or Venus, and that in the days of Jeremiah the people generally sacrificed to the queen of heaven, as they then called her, it may show the origin of and account for the presence of these amorous songs. See Jeremiah xliv. 15-30.

Probably none of these books were known to Nehemiah; they form no part of the Law and the Prophets, and they were undoubtedly placed in their present position at a much later period.

THE PROPHETS. — ISAIAH.

Many of the prophetical writings show the mark of the same pen that wrote the Law.

Nehemiah introduces the prophecies of Isaiah by the statement that they were written "in the days of Uzziah, Jotham, Ahaz, and Hezekiah, kings of Judah." The vision of Jehovah (6th chapter) occurred "in the year that King Uzziah died." In the 7th chapter Nehemiah recites the causes leading to Isaiah's assurance to Ahaz that Rezin and Pekah shall not prevail against Jerusalem. Then come prophecies against Assyria, Babylon,

Moab, Syria, Egypt, and Ethiopia, against Tyre and against Jerusalem. In the 36th and 37th chapters, Nehemiah gives an account of the interview between Rabshakeh, an officer of Sennacherib king of Assyria, with Eliakim, Shebna, and Joab, officers of King Hezekiah: and the appeal of Rabshakeh to the people, the appeal of Hezekiah to Isaiah, his prophecy, the message of Sennacherib, the prayer of Hezekiah, the message of Isaiah, and the death of Sennacherib according to Isaiah's prophecy.

The history is continued in the 38th chapter, in the record of the sickness of Hezekiah, the message of Isaiah, and the lengthening of his (Hezekiah's) days. In the 39th chapter Nehemiah continues the history of the times in connection with the acts of Isaiah, giving the letter of Merodach-baladan, king of Babylon, the indiscreet action of Hezekiah, and the prophecy of Isaiah against his house. This apparently ends the prophetic utterances of Isaiah. At the 40th chapter an unknown prophet appears who will be mentioned later.

JOEL and HOSEA's prophecies were uttered to the Israelites from twenty-five to forty years before the time that Isaiah warned Judah. AMOS also prophesies against Israel in the days of Jeroboam, son of Joash, king of Israel, "two years before the earthquake," which, Zechariah says, was "in the days of Uzziah, king of Judah." Thirty-five years after Amos and Hosea, MICAH prophesies; his utterances are against both Judah and Israel. NAHUM, thirty-five years later still, prophesies against Nineveh; HABAKKUK, nearly one hundred years later, against the Chaldæans, ZEPHANIAH against Judah, and OBADIAH against Edom.

JONAH.

Distinct from all the other prophetic writings is the book of Jonah. The books of the prophets from Isaiah to Malachi, excepting Jonah and Daniel, are full of promises, reproofs, and warnings to the Hebrews, of threats against and denunciations of the various peoples and nations with whom they came into contact.

Jonah, on the contrary, gives neither warnings to the Jews nor denunciations to other nations, except the message sent to Nineveh; the very nation against whom, a few years after, Isaiah and the other prophets hurl prophecies of destruction and annihilation.

The very full history of Assyria which we now have from her own records, contemporary with that of the Hebrew nation from David down to the destruction of Nineveh, shows that no such incident as that recorded in Jonah could have taken place.

The Ninevites had their own gods, whom they held in the highest esteem and reverence; several of them they believed were self-existent; they were endowed with the various powers and attributes of the Deity. Through their favor, the Assyrians, as a nation, obtained their victories, and by their love and care they enjoyed fruitful seasons and were protected from famine and pestilence.

At the date of Jonah it is doubtful if they had ever heard of Jehovah, the God of the Hebrews, and, if they had, it would only be to despise him, as the god of a small and insignificant nation, of whose power they had no fear; a nation, in fact, a portion of whom a few years after this date they made tributary to themselves, and still later destroyed, carrying their inhabitants captive to Assyria. There never was a time when they would have listened or paid attention to a message such as is represented as delivered by Jonah.

That being the case, what is the story, and what does it mean?

Apparently it is a parable, written to teach a lesson. With the Hebrews a miracle was a natural event. It was familiar to their minds from its daily occurrence in the early life of their nation, and its power had been shown in every exigency of their national existence, when they depended on Jehovah their God; and they would not hesitate to use such a power to illustrate a tale, or to point a moral lesson, as is done in this case.

This parable contains several lessons, needed not only by the Hebrews of that day, but lessons which the Christians of this day may lay to heart and profit by.

The first lesson shows God's individual knowledge of each man, and the duty laid upon him to perform. He cannot attempt to evade this work without danger to himself and to others. If in his misery, disobedience, and sin the man repents, then the Deity will bring him out of the depths, and give him another chance to fulfil his obligations.

The second is the power of and the answer to prayer. Then Jonah prayed unto the Lord his God out of the fish's belly; "I cried, by reason of my affliction, unto the Lord, and he heard me; out of the belly of hell cried I, and thou heardst my voice." "And the Lord spake unto the fish, and it vomited out Jonah upon the dry land."

The third is a lesson of toleration. The Jews believed that all mankind outside of their own race were enemies of Jehovah, and that he would willingly destroy them. In this story Jonah is represented as warning the *heathen* city; when the inhabitants repented, the Deity forgave them; and, in answer to Jonah's petulant remonstrance, he gives as a reason therefor, "should not I spare Nineveh, that great city, wherein are more than six score thousand persons *that cannot discern between their right hand and their left hand;* and also *much cattle?*"

He had compassion for the ignorant inhabitants who knew not his law, and even for the innocent cattle. Is this not a lesson also for so-called Christians who, by their intolerant bigotry, condemn the ignorant nations who know not God — who "cannot discern between their right hand and their left hand"— to eternal condemnation and torture because of their ignorance? *They* would not have saved Nineveh any more than would Jonah.

JEREMIAH.

The prominent figure in the last days of the Hebrew monarchy is Jeremiah; and Nehemiah gives us a history of the last twenty-five years of the life of Judah, so far as the events therein described make plain the actions and prophecies of Jeremiah. In so doing we obtain an insight into the character of the people, their disregard of and disbelief in Jehovah, their national God, and the difficulties and dangers surrounding, and the sufferings of the prophet, when carrying out the behests of Jehovah.

Nehemiah's introduction declares that Jeremiah commenced his work in the thirteenth year of the reign of Josiah, king of Judah, B.C. 628, and he continued until the eleventh year of Zedekiah, and the carrying away of Jerusalem captive, a period of forty years, extended a few years while in Egypt.

The first nineteen chapters contain warnings and admonitions and prophecies, addressed principally to Judah; they are without date, but were probably uttered during the reign of Josiah. These utterances of Jeremiah were not relished by the people in general, and conspiracies were formed against him, which resulted in the incidents mentioned in the twentieth chapter.

Pashur, the son of Immer the priest, smote Jeremiah and put him into the stocks. The next day, however, he released him. Jeremiah then prophesied against Jerusalem, and against Pashur and his house. At the same time he complained to Jehovah that "I am in derision daily, every one mocketh me."

In the beginning of the reign of Jehoiachim, the son of Josiah, the people became so incensed against Jeremiah because of his prophecies against Jerusalem that "the priests and the prophets and all the people took him, saying, Thou shalt surely die." He was brought before the princes of Judah and charged with prophesying against the city; he was, however, finally released.

In the fourth year of the reign of Jehoiachim, Jeremiah says that for ten years he has warned them "that the Lord hath sent unto you all his servants the prophets . . . but ye have not hearkened, nor inclined your ear to hear; therefore, he says, Nebuchadnezzar shall carry this people away captive, this whole land shall be a desolation and an astonishment, and these nations shall serve the king of Babylon seventy years." A list of these nations is then given, beginning with Egypt and ending with "all the kingdoms of the world which are upon the face of the earth." At another time he prophesies against Jehoiachim, that he shall be buried with the burial of an ass, and that his son shall be childless, and shall be carried away captive to Babylon, where he shall die.

After the King Jehoiachim, the queen, the eunuchs, the princes, and many of the people of Judah and Jerusalem had been carried captive to Babylon, Jeremiah sends to the Jews in Babylon a letter informing them that their captivity shall last seventy years.

In the early part of the reign of Zedekiah, who was placed on the throne by Nebuchadnezzar, under a charge of desertion, Jeremiah is seized, beaten, and put in prison in the house of Jonathan the scribe, from which he is removed by order of the king to the court of the prison in the king's house. At the accusation of the princes, he is removed from thence and lowered into a miry dungeon, after being loaded with chains, from which he is afterward released at the intercession of Ebed-melech, an Ethiopian eunuch, and is removed again to the court of the prison, but still kept in chains. The King Zedekiah then seeks a private interview with Jeremiah, and, upon swearing that he would not put him to death for his revelations, Jeremiah promises personal safety and the safety of the city if he shall deliver himself and city into the hands of the Chaldæans, but, if not, "then shall this city be given into the hands of the Chaldæans, and they shall burn it with fire, and thou shalt not escape out of their hand."

After the taking of Jerusalem by Nebuchadnezzar in B.C. 598, in the fourth year of the reign of Zedekiah, king of Judah, Hananiah, the son of Azur, the prophet, prophesies, "Thus speaketh the Lord, the God of Israel, saying, I have broken the yoke of the king of Babylon," and says that within two years the vessels of the Lord's house, the king with all the captives of Judah, shall come back to Jerusalem. He is rebuked by Jeremiah, and is told, "This year shalt thou die, because thou hast taught rebellion against the Lord," and the record is made that he "died the same year, in the seventh month."

In the ninth year of the reign of Zedekiah, Nebuchadnezzar laid siege to Jerusalem. At this time Jeremiah was still in prison. He continued to prophesy against Jerusalem and Zedekiah, but mingles with them promises of the restoration and the repeopling of the country. At this time, too, he prophesies against the Philistines, the Ammonites, the Edomites, and against Babylon.

"In the eleventh year of Zedekiah, king of Judah (B.C. 588), in the fourth month and ninth day of the month, the city was broken up." Zedekiah fled from the city, but was overtaken in the plains of Jericho. He was taken before Nebuchadnezzar, who slew his sons in his presence, put out his eyes, and carried him in chains to Babylon.

Nebuchadnezzar caused Jeremiah to be released from the court of the prison, removed his chains, and he returned to his home. Previous to doing this, Jeremiah saw Ebed-melech, through whose intercession he had been released from the loathsome dungeon, and promised him the protection of Jehovah.

The Chaldæans burned the king's house and the houses of the people with fire, and broke down the walls of Jerusalem. Then Nebuzar-adan, the captain of the guard, carried away captive into Babylon the remnant of the people that remained in the city, but he left of the poor of the people, which had nothing, in the land of Judah, and gave them vineyards and fields at the same time.

Nebuchadnezzar made Gedaliah governor over the people remaining in the land. He was afterwards slain by Ishmael, of the seed royal, who then fled to the Ammonites. The people then consulted Jeremiah as to what should be done, they promising to "obey the voice of the Lord our God." After prayer to God, Jeremiah delivers the message, promising them prosperity if they remained and served the king of Babylon, but if they decided to go to Egypt he threatens "that the sword which ye feared shall overtake you there in the land of Egypt, and there ye shall die."

The people then charge Jeremiah, "Thou speakest falsely; the Lord our God hath not sent thee to say, Go not into Egypt to sojourn there." The result is given in these words, "But Johanan the son of Kareah, and all the captains of the forces, took all the remnant of Judah that were returned from all nations, whither they had been driven, to dwell in the land of Judah; even men and women and children, and the king's daughters, and every person that Nebuzar-adan, the captain of the guard, had left with Gedaliah the son of Ahikam the son of Shaphan, and Jeremiah the prophet, and Baruch the son of Neriah; so they came into the land of Egypt, for they obeyed not the voice of the Lord. Thus came they even to Tahpanhes."

After their residence at Tahpanhes, the Jews burned incense to other gods, for which Jeremiah rebuked them, and prophesied that Egypt would be delivered into the hands of Nebuchadnezzar, and that the Jews who had fled there should be destroyed by the sword, by famine, and by pestilence.

EZEKIEL.

Ezekiel was a captive in Babylon. His prophecies are mostly in the shape of visions, and are against Jerusalem, Tyre, and Egypt; his time being contemporaneous with Jeremiah.

DANIEL.

Daniel is one of the sons of King Hezekiah, who, with three of his brothers, was carried captive to Babylon. Nehemiah gives us the incidents leading to their selection as attendants on the king; the danger of the wise men because they could not inform the king of the dream which he had forgotten; the offer of Daniel to reveal the dream and the interpretation thereof, resulting in the brothers being made rulers of the province of Babylon.

The remainder of the book appears to be transcripts of public documents; relating the throwing of three of the brothers into the burning fiery furnace, and their escape, Nebuchadnezzar's proclamation of his dream relating to himself, its interpretation by Daniel, the result, and his return to reason. These visions, together with those of Daniel, were considered of national importance, and were made matters of public record, and appear to have been copied *verbatim*, with such connecting statements as were necessary to a right understanding of the record. Daniel's life covered the seventy years of captivity and to the reign of Darius the Mede.

It is noticeable that the Deity in this book is spoken of as the "God of Heaven," "The most high God," and in Nebuchadnezzar's proclamation he is styled "God of gods;" thus giving him a place above all gods.

During the life of Daniel an unknown prophet appears, of whom we know nothing but his writings.

ISAIAH THE YOUNGER.

At the fortieth chapter of Isaiah, the old prophet ceases and this new one appears without introduction of any kind. His first words, "Comfort ye my people," are a key to the spirit of his writings.

This prophet without name might be called Isaiah the younger. His time is one hundred and fifty to two hundred years later than Isaiah, or about B.C. 550, and his standpoint is different. He is a dweller in Babylon and his utterances are of a joyful nature. He prophesies relief to the Jews through the downfall of Babylon, and names Cyrus as the instrument of God's will, through whom they will be released from bondage and be permitted to return to Judah. The temple will be rebuilt at Jerusalem, the worship of Jehovah restored, and the walls of the city be re-established.

In the utterances of this unknown prophet, Jehovah ceases to be the tutelary god of the Hebrews, standing on a par with the gods of the surrounding nations. He for the first time becomes the sole and only God of the universe, the creator and sustainer of all. "Thus saith the Lord, I am the first and I am the last; and beside me there is no God." "Thus saith God, the Lord, he that created the heavens and stretched them out; he that spread forth the earth and that which cometh out of it; he that giveth breath unto the people upon it, and spirit to them that walk therein." These avowals of the greatness and power of Jehovah are many times repeated, and appear only in the writings of this unknown prophet; they are entirely distinct from the older prophets, and there is a note of gladness and joy running through the whole of his utterances which separates him from all others.

HAGGAI prophesies after the return of the Jews to Jerusalem. About the same time ZECHARIAH issues his prophecies; both reprove and encourage the Jews.

At the ninth chapter Zechariah ceases, and another UNKNOWN PROPHET appears. He resides at Damascus, his time is nearly one hundred years earlier, or during the period of Jeremiah, and his utterances are against Jerusalem, Tyre, Sidon, and the Philistines.

MALACHI is the last of the prophets. He rebukes the priests of the restored worship in the new Jerusalem, and his time is during the governorship of Nehemiah, probably not far from B.C. 410. The Bible date is B.C. 397.

All the prophets at the time of and after the captivity speak more or less distinctly of the coming of the Christ, of his power and rule, and the extent and perpetuity of his government.

APPENDIX.

APPENDIX.

PROPHECY SUSTAINED.

Prophecies form a prominent and striking portion of the Hebrew Scriptures. Beginning with Abram, they are continued through the whole history of the Israelites. These predictions are both personal and national, affecting not only the Israelites but the nations also with whom they came in contact. The fulfilment of some of them is recorded in the Scriptures, and history records the accomplishment of others.

As it has been claimed that the prophecies in the Hebrew Scriptures against the surrounding nations were uttered at a point of time so near the occurrence of the events as to be easily foreseen, or that they were written out after the event had happened, and were then put into the mouths of these prophets, we have traced the fulfilment of some of them in the light of these statements; and herein will be found prophecies against Egypt, Assyria, and Babylon, and the particulars of their specific fulfilment or of their continued action until the present day, as taken from Assyrian records and from ancient and modern history.

EGYPT.

Isaiah prophesied, according to the Bible, from 760 to 712 B.C. German critics make his years from 740 to 710 B.C. They also claim that chapters 40 to 66 of the book of Isaiah were written by some other person, at a later period. We will therefore confine our selections to the portions that are unquestioned.

"Woe to the land shadowing with wings. . . . Behold, the Lord rideth upon a swift cloud and shall come into Egypt; and the idols of Egypt shall be moved at his presence, and the heart of Egypt shall melt in the midst of it, and I will set the Egyptians against the Egyptians, and they shall fight every one against his brother, and every one against his neighbor; city against city, and kingdom against kingdom; and the spirit of Egypt shall fail in the midst thereof . . . and the Egyptians will I give over into the hand of a cruel lord; and a fierce king shall rule over them, saith the Lord, the Lord of hosts." . . . "In that day shall Egypt be like unto women; and it shall be afraid and fear." . . . "So shall the Assyrian lead away the Egyptians prisoners, and the Ethiopians captives, young and old, naked and barefoot."

FULFILLED BY ASSUR-BANIPAL, KING OF ASSYRIA, B. C. 668.

This prophecy was literally fulfilled by Assurbanipal, son of Esarhaddon, king of Assyria, forty years after the death of Isaiah. Assur-banipal, in 668

B.C., attacked and routed the Egyptian army at Karbanit, and marched on to Memphis; the king of Egypt fled. Many of the petty kings of the country joined the victorious army and aided the Assyrians. Thus brother fought against brother, neighbor against neighbor, city against city, and kingdom against kingdom. Three several times was the Assyrian yoke thrown off, and as often did Assur-banipal reconquer the country. On the last occasion, about B.C. 665, the Assyrians wreaked their vengeance on the city of Thebes.[1] "No city in the world had such a series of public monuments; the temples, statues, obelisks, and palaces, the work of ages during the glory of Egypt, were now, as far as possible, disfigured and destroyed. The Assyrians carried away silver and gold, precious stones, the furniture of the palace, robes of various materials, horses, people, male and female, elephants and monkeys. Two of the great obelisks were taken to Nineveh as trophies; the Assyrians boasted that they swept the city like a flood, and the army returned from Egypt laden with spoil."

Jeremiah, B.C. 629 to 587 (Chadwick says 626 to 584 B.C.), writes, "Thus saith the Lord: Behold, I will give Pharaoh-Hophra, king of Egypt, into the hand of his enemies, and into the hand of them that seek his life." . . . "The Lord of hosts, the God of

---

[1] To George Smith's works, Assyria from the Earliest Times to the Fall of Nineveh, and History of Babylon, I am indebted for most of the facts relating to the actions of the Assyrian and Babylonian monarchs.

Israel, saith, Behold, I will punish the multitude of No, and Pharaoh and Egypt, with their gods and their kings, even Pharaoh, and all them that trust in him; and I will deliver them into the hand of those that seek their lives, and into the hand of Nebuchadnezzar, king of Babylon, and into the hand of his servants, . . . and when he cometh he shall smite the land of Egypt, and deliver such as are for death to death, and such as are for captivity to captivity, and such as are for the sword to the sword, and I will kindle a fire in the houses of the gods of Egypt; and he shall burn them and carry them away captives; and he shall array himself with the land of Egypt, as a shepherd putteth on his garment." . . . "He shall break also the images of Beth-shemesh, that is in the land of Egypt; and the houses of the gods of the Egyptians shall he burn with fire."

FULFILLED BY NEBUCHADNEZZAR, KING OF BABYLON, B. C. 572.

"B.C. 572, twelve or fifteen years after the death of Jeremiah, Nebuchadnezzar, king of Babylon, marched in person into Egypt, and, defeating the army of Hophra, overran the country and plundered it of all its wealth." Hophra fell into his hands, and was deposed, a general named Ahmes or Amasis being acknowledged as king of Egypt in his stead, the new monarch being installed as a vassal of Babylonia.

Ezekiel, B.C. 595 to 574, prophesies, "Son of man,

take up a lamentation for Pharaoh, king of Egypt, and say unto him: Thus saith the Lord God, I will therefore spread out my net over thee with a company of many people; and they shall bring thee up in my net. Then will I leave thee upon the land, I will cast thee forth upon the open field, and will cause all the fowls of the heaven to remain upon thee, and I will fill the beasts of the whole earth with thee; and I will lay thy flesh upon the mountains, and fill the valleys with thy height. I will also water with thy blood the land wherein thou swimmest, even to the mountains." . . . "For thus saith the Lord God: The sword of the king of Babylon shall come upon thee; by the swords of the mighty will I cause thy multitude to fall, the terrible of the nations, all of them: and they shall spoil the pomp of Egypt, and all the multitude thereof shall be destroyed."

FULFILLED BY CAMBYSES, THE KING OF PERSIA, B. C. 525.

B.C. 525, fifty years after the death of Ezekiel, Cambyses, son of Cyrus the Persian, who conquered Babylon, proceeded against Egypt, and it fell into his hands. The adjacent tribes of Libyans, with the Greeks of Barca and Cyrene, also submitted to his arms. The Egyptians had made a stubborn resistance;—Psammenitus the king was executed by order of Cambyses, whose armies ravaged the country, and the land was watered with the blood of the Egyptians. The vengeance of the Persian was terrible.

Even now the means by which he accomplished his desolating work is a problem; but under him the prophecies were fulfilled, the idols were destroyed, and the images ceased out of Noph.

For more than one hundred years Egypt remained a Persian possession, a province of the empire. About B.C. 414, the Persians were driven out, and for about sixty years Egypt was again governed by native rulers.

But Ezekiel had prophesied, "There shall be there a base kingdom. It shall be the basest of kingdoms; neither shall it exalt itself any more above the nations; for I will diminish them that they shall no more rule over the nations . . . and there shall be no more a prince of the land of Egypt."

About B.C. 350, Artaxerxes III. (Ochus) reconquered Egypt. He "re-enacted the scenes attributed to Cambyses, but with a bloodthirstiness and cruelty of his own, and, having completely crushed out the last seeds of rebellion, returned to Susa with an enormous booty."

B.C. 332, Alexander the Great having overcome the Persians, Egypt became a Grecian province. Here he founded Alexandria as the capital of the world. For three centuries Egypt was under Grecian rule, which then gave way to Rome.

B.C. 30, Egypt became a department of the great Roman Empire, and so continued for nearly seven hundred years.

A.D. 639, Egypt came under Mohammedan sway,

and from that time has been a possession of the Turk.

From the conquest of Egypt by Artaxerxes, B.C. 350, to the present time, a period of over twenty-two hundred years, the sceptre has gone from Egypt; it has been subject to foreign sway. It has been "the basest of kingdoms," it has been "diminished," the land has been "laid waste by strangers," and there has been "no more a prince of the land of Egypt."

Egypt, the oldest, had been the most powerful empire in the world. There was the seat of luxury and learning. Her history extended back so far that her beginning was unknown. The first glimpses we have of her show her well advanced in all the arts of civilization. Iron, steel, bronze, gold, and silver were used in the mechanic arts. Painting, music, and sculpture were studied. Their architecture was massive, their structures stupendous. They excelled in the manufacture of linen; costly furniture, rich with coverings of gold cloth, adorned their houses. They were expert potters, glass-blowers, and carpenters, and astronomy and medicine were carefully studied.

When Isaiah uttered his prophecies, Egypt was in the height of her power, and a long time after (B.C. 610) she aided in the downfall of Assyria; she exulted in her strength and in the power of her arms.

If we examine these prophecies, and the records of the Assyrians, Babylonians, and Persians, we see how accurate was the prediction to the facts, as stated in these records, of events taking place from fifteen to seventy years afterward. Egypt was not to be destroyed, but to remain in existence, the basest of kingdoms, without native rulers forever.

The Turkish Empire is tottering to its fall. In its destruction the nations of Europe will divide the spoils. Egypt will come under Christian sway and influences, and the native Egyptian race be blotted out of political existence forever.

ASSYRIA.

Of Assyria it was foretold by Isaiah, "It shall cease among the nations." Fifty years before the days of Isaiah, Shalmanezer, king of Assyria, received tribute from Jehu, king of Israel. Pul, or Tiglath Pileser II., who reigned about the time of Isaiah, received from Menahem, king of Israel, one thousand talents of silver as tribute, as recorded in Second Kings. The Assyrian had extended his government to and received tribute also from the Medes, Tyre, Sidon, Damascus, and Idumea, and his empire at that time also included Babylon. At this time it is that Isaiah declares, "It shall come to pass that when the Lord hath performed his whole work upon Mount Zion and upon Jerusalem, I will punish the fruit of the stout heart of the king of Assyria, and the glory of his high looks;" again, "I will break the Assyrian in my hand, and upon my mountains tread him under foot." "Through the voice of the Lord shall the Assyrian be beaten down." "He shall flee from

THE DESTRUCTION OF NINEVEH.

the sword, and his young men shall be discomfited. He shall pass over to his stronghold for fear, and his princes shall be afraid."

Micah, B.C. 750, says, "They shall waste the land of Assyria with the sword, and the land of Nimrod in the entrance thereof."

Nahum, about 715 B.C. (Chadwick, B.C. 630), says, "But with an overflowing flood will he make an utter end of the place thereof.". The manner in which the place should be taken is indicated. "The defence shall be prepared. The gates of the rivers shall be opened, and the palace shall be dissolved." Again, "Thy people in the midst of them are women, the gates of thy land shall be set wide open unto thine enemies; the fire shall devour thy bars." "Then shall the fire devour thee, the sword shall cut thee off. Thy crowned are as the locusts, and thy captains as the great grasshoppers which camp in the hedges in the cold day, but when the sun riseth they flee away, and their place is not known where they are." "Take ye the spoil of silver, take the spoil of gold, for there is none end of the store and glory out of all the pleasant furniture. She is empty and void and waste, and the heart melteth, and the knees smite together, and much pain is in all loins, and the faces of them all gather blackness;" "Thy nobles shall dwell in the dust, thy people are scattered upon the mountains and no man gathereth them; there is no healing of thy bruises."

Zephaniah, B.C. 712 to 680 (Chadwick, 630), says,

"He will stretch out his hands against the north and destroy Assyria, and will make Nineveh a desolation and dry like a wilderness, . . . and flocks shall lie down in the midst of her, all the beasts of the nations; both the cormorant and the bittern shall lodge in the upper lintels of it, their voice shall sing in the windows, desolation shall be in the thresholds, for he shall uncover the cedar work." "This is the rejoicing city that dwelt carelessly, that said in her heart, I am, and there is none beside me; how is she become a desolation, a place for beasts to lie down in."

About the time of these first prophecies Assyria had overthrown the kingdom of Israel, and at two separate times had carried portions of the inhabitants away captive. Finally Sargon, B.C. 721, completed the capture of Israel and carried the citizens of Samaria away captive.

B.C. 700, Sennacherib invaded Judah, took forty-six fenced cities, and carried 200,150 of the inhabitants into captivity. These cities he separated from Judah and divided them among the neighboring kings. He then captured Lachish, one of the last remaining strong cities of Judah, and from thence dictated terms to Hezekiah, the humbled king of Judah; receiving "a forced tribute of thirty talents of gold, eight hundred talents of silver, and precious stones of various sorts, couches and thrones of ivory, skins and horns of buffaloes, girls and eunuchs, male and female musicians, together with horses, mules, asses, camels, oxen, and sheep, in great numbers."

SENNACHERIB BUILDS NINEVEH.

Nineveh was made the royal city by Sennacherib, who repaired and rebuilt it until it became a city "splendid as the sun." Three hundred and sixty thousand men, captives taken in war, were employed in building it, very possibly some or many of the Hebrew captives were so employed. He erected the new palace of Koyunjik, which covered more than eight acres of ground and was ornamented with great splendor. The city formed a quadrangle of sixty miles surrounded by walls one hundred feet high, broad enough at top for three chariots to drive abreast, and defended by fifteen hundred towers, each two hundred feet high. Within were palaces, structures by the side of whose gigantic proportions the grandeurs of Greek and Roman architecture are dwarfed into insignificance, in whose halls kings had feasted and revelled, and in which he had received the tribute of distant nations.

Esarhaddon, the younger son of Sennacherib, succeeded his father B.C. 681. He "rebuilt the walls of Babylon, which had been destroyed by his father, raised again the temple of Bel, returned the various images of the gods which his father had carried to Assyria, and restored to the Babylonians the plunder of their cities; and, proclaiming himself king of Babylon as well as Assyria, passed much of his time in his southern capital."

About B.C. 670, the whole of Palestine and the surrounding country submitted to Esarhaddon. In the list of twelve kings who submitted to his sway was Manasseh, king of Judah, whom he bound and brought captive to Babylon.

A few years afterward he conquered the Medes, then Arabia, and finally Egypt.

It was during his reign that the predictions of Nahum and Zephaniah were uttered.

Assur-banipal succeeded his father Esarhaddon, B.C. 668, and reigned forty-two years. In the latter years of his reign he exerted himself in ornamenting and beautifying Nineveh. He enriched it with spoils of countless cities. His conquering arms had drawn tribute from all nations. Thousands of captives were at his command, and were employed in building his palaces and other works. He patronized the arts, established schools and colleges, collected in his Halls of Record, or Library, at Koyunjik, the extensive literature of a race far advanced in civilization before the flood. These records consisted of clay tablets and cylinders on which were stamped, while soft, the wedge-shaped or cuneiform characters, which, being hardened in the fire, were easily handled and read.

At this time Nineveh was the most splendid and the richest city on the earth; its king was ruler of the civilized world. According to Chadwick's date, the most particular and distinct predictions of the fate of Nineveh were uttered by the prophets at this time, when Assyria was at the height of its power as here described, and twenty-four years before their accomplishment.

Bel-zakir-iskun, about B.C. 626, was probably the next Assyrian monarch, but little is known of his reign. Being threatened by the king of Egypt on one side, and the Median king on the other, while Babylon had thrown off the yoke of servitude, he acted with great vigor. He raised two armies; one he committed to the care of Nabopolassar, with orders to reconquer Babylon and protect the region of the Persian Gulf, while he himself proceeded against the king of Media. Nabopolassar was successful, as was his royal master for a time, but the Assyrian monarch was finally driven back, and the Median king followed him with the intention of besieging Nineveh. This enterprise was checked by an irruption of Scythians, who crossed the Caucasus in great numbers, and overran Assyria, Media, and Syria. The dominion of the Scythians lasted many years, but they were finally driven out, and the government reverted to the former rulers.

About B.C. 610, Nabopolassar, the tributary king of Babylon, resolved to overthrow the Assyrian power, by alliances with Necho, king of Egypt, and Cyaxares, king of the Medes. About B.C. 609, the war commenced, and the Assyrian king, after defeating his enemies in three pitched battles, was obliged, by the continual accessions to the enemy's forces, to retreat to and shut himself up in Nineveh. The siege of Nineveh by the combined forces lasted over two years, the walls of the city, a hundred feet high and fifty feet thick, keeping out the enemy and foiling all their attempts to scale or breach them.

In the third year there was an extraordinary rise of the Tigris River, and the flood carried away a considerable portion of the wall of the city. On the subsiding of the flood, the besieging host entered by the breach and took the city. The Assyrian monarch, seeing that all was lost, gathered his wives and valuables into his palace, and, setting it on fire, perished in the flames.

The allied armies swept the city with the sword; and, after plundering it of all its gold and silver and jewels, the accumulation of centuries of aggressive and successful war, they destroyed its walls and reduced its palaces to ashes. Nineveh was no more; and Assyria ceased to exist as a separate nation. So thorough was the destruction of the city that even the site of it was lost, and for ages unknown.

Nineveh became "a desolation and dry like a wilderness." The destruction of the dam across the Tigris, and of the elaborate methods of irrigation, produced this result. For generations "the flocks of the Arabs have lain down in the midst of her."

Layard's description of the Arabs and their flocks, his account of the desert aspect of the region during the summer heats, fulfil the prophecy, "She is empty and void and waste." The researches of Layard show that it was by fire the palaces were destroyed. The prophecies respecting her downfall were fulfilled to the letter. Diodorus says, "The river, swollen with the rains, overflowed and carried away twenty furlongs of the walls. Then the king, frightened by the apprehension that an old prophecy, that the city should not be captured till the river became its enemy, was now fulfilled, built in his palace a large funeral pile, and burnt himself, his concubines, his wealth, and his palace to the ground. The enemy, meanwhile, entering by the breach in the walls, captured the city." Thus with an "overflowing flood" was "an utter end" made of Nineveh's glory, while the "fire devoured her," and the "sword cut her off."

Thus were the prophecies by various prophets, uttered from twenty-four to one hundred and forty years before, literally fulfilled, and the words used in the prophetic denunciations by Isaiah, Nahum, and Zephaniah give the best descriptions of the actual events.

BABYLON.

Of Babylon, that great, that mighty city, whose name became a synonyme for colossal pride, power, and licentiousness, — the downfall was pronounced by some of the same prophets that predicted the downfall of Nineveh. This city figures largely in the prophetic utterances of the Hebrews. The country was for many years the place of their captivity, and it was the native country of Abram, whom they claimed as their ancestor.

The Bible credits Nimrod with being the founder of Babylon, but the early records claim it as being a city before the flood. Berosus, a native historian, possessed apparently authentic records dating back to about 2300 years B.C. He gives a mythical period of 34,080 years during which eighty-six kings reigned, down to a time when the country was conquered by the Medes, who reigned two hundred and twenty-four years.

In the early times there appear to have been several districts, each with its capital city and separate rule. The first mentioned in the inscriptions is "Ur," earlier known as "Nipur," the birthplace of Abram. Another capital city was Karrak, a third was Larsa. A king named Kuder-mabuk conquered the country which he called Lower Babylonia. Kuder-mabuk was afterward overcome by Hammurabi, ruler of Upper Babylonia, thus uniting the whole country under one rule.

Although Assyria was the child of Babylon, the child gradually outstripped the mother, and for several hundred years Babylonia, with fitful exceptions, was subject to Assyria.

In the division of the spoil at the taking of Nineveh, by the armies of Egypt, Media, and Babylonia, about B.C. 607, the southern portion of Assyria and a portion of Arabia fell to the king of Babylon. The sudden extinction of the Assyrian Empire relieved many of the smaller governments from the rule that had dominated for hundreds of years, and three apparently nearly equal powers took the place of Assyria: Egypt on the south, Media on the east, and Babylonia in the centre.

B.C. 605, Nabopolassar, king of Babylonia, became engaged in a discussion with Necho, king of Egypt, respecting boundaries, which soon led to hostilities. Entering into the war with vigor, he placed his son Nebuchadnezzar in command of his armies, who suddenly attacked and routed the Egyptians at Carchemish, gaining thereby the control of all Syria, through which he marched unopposed; receiving the submission and tribute of the various petty kings and princes, to the borders of Egypt; among these was Jehoiachim, king of Judah, who had been placed on the throne by Necho, king of Egypt, but was now forced to submit to the Babylonian yoke. While on this expedition Nabopolassar died, and Nebuchadnezzar returned to Babylon to assume the government.[1]

B.C. 602, Jehoiachim revolted against Babylon, and in B.C. 598 Nebuchadnezzar swept down upon Palestine. Jehoiachim had died, and his son Jehoiachin had ascended the throne. Nebuchadnezzar dethroned him, and placed his uncle Zedekiah on the throne, carrying Jehoiachin and numerous other captives with him to Babylon.[2]

[1] The Bible date is B.C. 606.
[2] Mr. Chadwick says that the Jews were in captivity but fifty years, instead of seventy years, as prophesied by Jeremiah.

Jeremiah's prophecy is against "this land and against the inhabitants thereof and against (not the Hebrews only, but against) all these nations round about . . . and *these nations shall serve the king of Babylon* (not by captivity, but by paying tribute) seventy years."

We have shown above that, B.C. 605, Nabopolassar received the

At the time of his death, B.C. 562, Nebuchadnezzar was master of the western world; he had reigned forty years; while carrying on his wars he had also employed himself in increasing the magnificence and grandeur of Babylon. "He rebuilt the great temple dedicated to Bel, and adorned it with gold and precious stones. He raised again the tower, called the foundation of heaven and earth. The sanctuary of Bel he roofed with cedar brought from Lebanon, and overlaid it with gold;" he also rebuilt or restored the temple of the moon-god, "the temples of the sun, of Val, and of the goddess Gula; the temple of Ishtar or Venus, and other buildings," and, to please his wife, a Median princess, he built the celebrated Hanging Gardens, with arched terraces which were carried to a height overtopping the walls of the city, were covered with earth, and irrigated by water raised from the Euphrates by machinery. In this garden grew all manner of trees and plants to delight the eyes and gratify the taste. He enriched the city with the spoils of other nations; he rebuilt the walls

submission of the king of Judah, and *all the nations round about*, from which time they served the king of Babylon as vassal nations. Nebuchadnezzar carried the king and a large number of the inhabitants of Judah captive to Babylon, and to these Jeremiah sends a letter, informing them of the length of their captivity.

Ezra records that, B.C. 536, Cyrus issued a proclamation for the return of the Jews to Jerusalem, and the next year, B.C. 535, they "laid the foundation of the temple of the Lord," just seventy years from the commencement of their servitude.

By the overthrow of Babylon the surrounding nations also were relieved from their subjection to the Babylonian king; these nations were Edom, Moab, Ammon, Tyre, Sidon, and others.

of the city, and in every way increased its magnificence and strength, and we can well credit the words put into his mouth by the Hebrew chronicler, "Is not this great Babylon that I have built for the house of the kingdom, by the might of my power and for the honor of my majesty?"

Nebuchadnezzar had made Babylon so magnificent that it was known as Babylon the Great. Herodotus reports it as a "large, wealthy, important, and populous city;" he describes it as "fifteen miles square, sixty miles in circumference, enclosing two hundred and twenty-five square miles, with walls of brick cemented with bitumen, three hundred feet high, and eighty-seven feet thick at top, the Euphrates flowing through the city and dividing it into two parts. In the circuit of the walls were one hundred gates of brass with brazen lintels and door-posts. There was an inner wall enclosing the city proper, with walls also at the river's bank, and in these walls were brazen gates fronting the principal streets, which were one hundred and fifty feet wide and crossing each other at right angles. When the gates were shut, there was no entrance into the city proper from the river, and a hostile force would be shut in between the parallel walls that lined it, and at the mercy of the besieged." All these mighty works were erected by the hundreds of thousands of captives brought back by the king in his various wars.

The earliest prophecies of the fall of Babylon were made by Isaiah, 760 to 712 B.C.

Jeremiah (Chadwick says his time was 626 to 584 B.C.) wrote while Nebuchadnezzar was ruler of all the eastern world and Egypt, and at least fifty years before the taking of Babylon by Cyrus. When Nebuchadnezzar said in his pride, "Is not this great Babylon that I have built?" was there anything in this almost universal empire, this great prosperity, that could lead a contemporary to prophesy calamity? Nay, was it not very improbable that such a strange fate, so specifically described, should overtake this great, this magnificent city? How improbable that a capital like this should become utterly deserted and desolate!

Isaiah, speaking in the name of Jehovah, says, "I will stir up the Medes against them, which shall not regard silver, and as for gold they shall not delight in it." Jeremiah says, "Out of the north there cometh up a nation against her." ... "I will raise and cause to come up against Babylon an assembly of great nations from the north country, and Chaldea shall be a spoil." ... "Behold, a people shall come from the north, and a great nation, and many kings shall be raised up from the coasts of the earth." These statements are repeated with slight variations. Even the time when the overthrow should take place is mentioned.

Jeremiah speaks of Nebuchadnezzar's conquests, and the subjection of the neighboring kingdoms to his power, and, in the name of Jehovah, says, "I have given all these lands into the hands of Nebuchadnezzar, king of Babylon. All nations shall serve him and his son and his son's son (or descendants) until the very time of his land come, and then many nations and great kings shall serve themselves of him." In another passage he says, "These nations shall serve the king of Babylon seventy years, and it shall come to pass when seventy years are accomplished that I will punish the king of Babylon, and that nation, saith Jehovah, for their iniquity."

Herodotus informs us that for fifteen or twenty years Cyrus the Persian had been at war against various nations, and in the spring of 538 B.C. he led his conquering legions to the plains of Babylon. For this undertaking he had swelled his forces from distant nations and many different people. The armies of these subjugated nations were incorporated with those of the Medes and Persians, and they approached Babylon from the north.

The leader of the invading host was designated by Isaiah the younger, "Thus saith the Lord to his anointed, to Cyrus, whose right hand I have holden to subdue all nations before him." . . .

. . . "I will open before him the two-leaved gates, and the gates of brass shall not be shut. . . . I will give thee the treasures of darkness, and hidden riches of secret places, that thou mayest know that I the Lord, which call thee by thy name, am the God of Israel."

The fulfilment of these prophecies seemed impossible, yet they came to pass, and the method by which they were accomplished is also foretold. "A drought is upon the waters and they shall be dried up. . . . I will make drunk her princes and her wise men and her mighty men, that they may rejoice and sleep a perpetual sleep and not awake."

A battle was fought before the walls, and the Persians obtained the victory; the Babylonians retreated to the city, and Cyrus immediately commenced the siege. The city was invulnerable to attack, and for full two years the siege continued. The Babylonians had laid up vast quantities of provision, and the extent of ground within the walls was so great, they could raise crops sufficient to support its inhabitants.

Confident and secure, they derided the invader from their walls. Their pride was excessive, they made light of the siege, and the king and his nobles passed the time in revelry and feasting. We have a picture in Daniel of the feast in which Belshazzar with a thousand of his lords participated on the very night in which Babylon was taken.

Herodotus says, "As they were engaged in festival, they continued dancing and revelling. . . . The vigilance of the guards was relaxed. The court and the people were lulled into false security, the river gates were left open. Cyrus turned off the water of the Euphrates into the artificial lake above. Had the Babylonians been apprised of what Cyrus had done, they could have closed the gates of the inner city, and, mounting the walls on both sides of the stream, would have caught the enemy in a trap and annihilated them. But the gates were open, the enemy entered, and the slaughter began. Owing to the vast size of the city, the inhabitants of the inner city knew nothing of the taking of the outer portions until the enemy were upon them."

Jeremiah's prophecy gives us a description of what actually took place. "A sword is upon the Chaldeans and upon the inhabitants of Babylonia, and upon her princes and upon her wise men, upon her horses and upon her chariots, and upon all the mingled people that are in the midst of her, and they shall become as women; a sword is upon her treasures, and they shall be robbed."

The riches of Babylon were immense; the spoils of many years of war and the tribute of nations had been poured into it. It had been the centre of the world's commerce and industry, and vast wealth had been accumulated, much of which was "hidden in secret places." The temples were highly ornamented and enriched with gold, silver, and precious stones, and many of their gods were made of solid gold. Their fate was foretold. "Bel boweth down, Nebo stoopeth, their idols were upon the beasts, they could not deliver the burden, but themselves are gone into captivity. . . . Babylon is fallen, and all the graven images of her gods he hath broken unto the ground, and they also became the prey of the conqueror."

Babylon was not to be suddenly destroyed as was Nineveh. "I will punish Bel in Babylon. . . . The nations shall not flow together any more unto her. . . . Babylon shall sink, and shall not rise from the evil that I will bring upon her. . . . Come down and sit in the dust, O virgin daughter of Babylon, sit on the ground. There is no throne, O daughter of the Chaldeans; sit thou silent, get thee into darkness, for thou shalt no more be called the lady of kingdoms."

Cyrus removed the seat of empire to Shushan, and Babylon began to decay.

Alexander the Great held court in Babylon B.C. 324.

His successor, Seleucus I., B.C. 312, took the materials from Babylon to build the city of Seleucia, on the banks of the Tigris.

About B.C. 140, it was taken by the Parthians, and Ctesiphon was founded on the opposite side of the river.

In the first century of the Christian era, although much reduced, it still contained a population of six hundred thousand.

In A.D. 114, it became the possession of the Romans, again in A.D. 199, and again in A.D. 363 under Julian.

About this time Gibbon says, "The adjacent pastures were covered with flocks and herds. The park was replenished with pheasants, peacocks, ostriches, roebucks, and wild boars. Nine hundred and sixty elephants were maintained for the use of the king. Six thousand guards successively mounted before the palace gates, and treasures of gold, silver, gems, silks, and aromatics were deposited in a hundred subterranean vaults."

Isaiah had said, "Babylon, the glory of kingdoms, the beauty of the Chaldees' excellency, shall be as when God overthrew Sodom and Gomorrah. It shall never be inhabited, neither shall it be dwelt in from generation to generation; neither shall the Arabian pitch his tent there; neither shall the shepherds make their fold there, but wild beasts of the desert shall lie there; and their houses shall be full of doleful creatures: and owls shall dwell there, and satyrs shall dance there, and the wild beasts of the islands shall cry in their desolate houses, and dragons in their pleasant palaces."

At a somewhat later date, "the great towns at the north of Babylon, which had succeeded to its wealth and fortunes, formed, so to speak, one street of twenty-eight miles."

About A.D. 650, the country fell into the hands of the Mohammedans, who erected a capital for their new empire at Bagdad. The materials for building were largely taken from Seleucia and Ctesiphon, which had fallen into ruins, these materials having been previously taken from Babylon.

During these events the decay of Babylon had been rapid, and finally the water of the Euphrates, no longer kept within bounds by embankments, poured over the level plain, and transformed it into malarial swamps. Temples, palaces, and mansions of brick became masses of ruins. The whole plain became the seat of virulent disease. The canals, being choked or broken, ceased to irrigate the land, and the former fruitful plain became arid and waste, the home only of the wandering Arab.

Layard describes the plain as covered with a perfect net-work of ancient canals and water-courses. "The face of the country," he says, "is dotted over with mounds and shapeless heaps, the remains of ancient towns and villages. On all sides fragments of glass, marble, pottery, and inscribed brick strew the ground. Owls start from the scanty thickets, and jackals skulk through the furrows. For mile after mile the track winds around and between low mounds, shapeless heaps of brick and rubbish. Babylon is tenantless and desolate. The Arabs will not pitch their tents there because they say it is haunted by evil spirits, which they dread more than they do wild animals, which they say also abound there." In fact, the prophecies themselves give the best description of the present condition of Babylon the great, the mighty, the powerful, the golden city. Isaiah says, "Wild beasts of the desert shall lie there." . . . "I will make it a possession for the bittern and pools of water, . . . a dwelling-place for dragons, an astonishment and a hissing." Thus are the prophecies fulfilled to the letter, yet not until ten or twelve centuries after their utterance.

. . . . .

We have thus shown the specific fulfilment of the various prophetical utterances respecting the greatest nations that came in contact with the Hebrew nation. These prophecies were uttered by many prophets, at times covering a period of four hundred years. In the case of Egypt, so far as they were immediate, they were fulfilled by Assyrian, Babylonian, and Persian kings, at times hundreds of years apart; the remaining predictions are still in force, and in continual process.

Assyria was suddenly blotted out of existence, and even the site of its great city Nineveh was forgotten; yet, when found, its appearance was particularly and truthfully described by the original prophecies.

Babylon was not to be destroyed at once. The manner of its taking was foretold, and was accomplished, but that did not complete the prophecies. It was gradually to be diminished, and we find it took twelve hundred years to accomplish the work; and the present appearance of ancient Babylon answers to the prophetic description.

Through the Hebrew people the Deity, by miracle and by prophecy, was making himself known to man. Mankind were reached and influenced by the senses only. An event out of the common course, they at once accredited to the power of a god. It was the direct act of a being higher and greater than a human being. This power was used in releasing the Israelites from the bondage in Egypt. Nebuchadnezzar acknowledged the power of the God of the Hebrews while they were in Babylonian captivity, and through his proclamation other nations were made aware of his being and power.

In the fulfilment of the predictions of the prophets,

the foreknowledge and the overruling power of Jehovah in the affairs and destiny of nations were made known. As these predictions, made in his name, were one after another accomplished, the Jews, and through them other nations, became aware of the greatness and majesty of Jehovah, and looked upon him with awe and reverence.

Among Christians, these evidences of the power and majesty of the Deity have been and are received with full faith by trusting hearts, and they have believed and do believe that God saw and knew everything from the beginning, and that he overrules all things for good.

It is only within the last hundred years that men have arisen who have thrown doubt upon the reality of miracles and upon the truths of prophecy.

Because man has so far advanced as to need no such supernatural proofs of the existence of God, and of his constant oversight and care, they reason that such proofs were never necessary, and therefore could not have been, and, forgetting that it is through the teachings of the Christ that they have arrived at that high state of being, they even belittle or deny him.

The truth is, it is useless for a disbeliever in the supernatural to attempt to understand the Bible. The book is a history of the supernatural. There is hardly a writer that does not record it. The Hebrew nation was born and cradled in the supernatural; in its youth it was led and strengthened by it; in its culmination it was supported by it, and in its death it was accompanied by it. The nation was brought into being for a special purpose and object; that purpose was carried out, that object attained; and, when attained, the nation thus supernaturally brought into being and supported ceased to exist.

The Bible contains a record of the instrumentalities through which God, the spiritual being, communicated with man, his child, also spiritual (but in this world encased in the natural, and while here subject to natural laws), enabling him by reason of his spiritual nature to comprehend the communications made, and to realize, to a limited degree, his own affinity to the Infinite Father.

These communications, commencing with man in his lowest spiritual state, and gradually advancing to fuller and greater revelations as he was able to receive and comprehend them, were accompanied through the whole by supernatural occurrences which we call miracles, intended to impress, not only the nation that was the recipient and witness of them, but, through it, to claim the attention of other nations, who, equally ignorant, were thereby made cognizant of the greatness and power of Jehovah; until, in process of time, mankind were ready to receive the full revelation of the being, power, character, purposes, and requirements of the Deity, as made known through Jesus the Christ, the consecrated messenger for whose coming and teaching all this preparation had been made.[1]

[1] In "Aryas, Semites and Jews," these revelations are traced and the gradual spiritual progress shown.

What are these supernatural exhibitions which we call miracles, but exhibitions of the power and majesty of the Almighty?

In the spiritual childhood of man these powers were shown in acts of injury and death, even as in the natural world the lightning injures and destroys. In later years, as man advanced, these same powers were exhibited in deeds of benevolence and love. To-day they are placed in the hands not of one man alone, but in the hands of thousands. Instead of one man alleviating the sickness, pain, and distress of the hundreds of Judea, thousands, by their increased knowledge of chemistry and of the healing art, are enabled to control disease, alleviate distress, and by their anæsthesia remove pain from millions all over the world.

It is only within the last hundred years that man has advanced sufficiently, spiritually and intellectually, to receive the mighty powers which God is now placing in his hands. The sun paints his pictures, and children play with the wonders of photography. The lightning, his former dreaded enemy, is now bound with metal bands and compelled to do his will. The various powers of the universe, before shown in the limited way we have mentioned, are now being placed in his hands, that they may minister to his well-being.

Man uses these latent powers of the universe to create new varieties of fruits, flowers, fowl, and animals. The chemistry of the sun, earth, air, and sea;

the powers of nature, hidden since the creation of the world, are now being brought to light and controlled by him, and, as he continues to spiritually advance, new and still greater powers, now unthought of, will doubtless become his allies; and yet man does not realize that he is using some of the tremendous powers which in their earlier crude shape he calls miracles.

God places these powers in the hands of thousands, and they cease to be miracles; and yet what does man know of electricity? he has found out a few of the laws governing it, and is thus enabled to use it for his benefit, and he looks forward to still greater power to be obtained in the future; but even the present powers would have been miraculous a few hundred years since.

In the pride of his knowledge, man says, to-day, "There is no such thing as miracle." He scouts the healing and beneficent miracles of the Christ, and the injurious and murderous powers of Moses. He can look back a few hundred years to the blackness of spiritual ignorance then existing, but cannot look back three thousand years and imagine the total darkness of the spiritual sense at that time. God places his powers in the hands of man at this time with lavish freedom, because, in his immense advance, he can understand them in part, and use them. But three thousand years ago the Deity could only reach man through the evidence of his senses, and that not in acts of love and beneficence; they would not have been appreciated. Exhibitions of power and strength, the ability to injure and destroy, were the only exhibitions that would reach, not the hearts, but the fears of man.

Let man gradually work back and see the spiritually ignorant hordes of Hebrew slaves, and the equally ignorant millions of Egypt, and ask himself in what other way could the Deity have given to these darkened minds evidences of his power that would have been understood. Evidences of injurious and destructive powers were the only means by which to reach these feeble and darkened minds. By denying the truth of these miracles, men blunt their own powers of perception, and blindly disown the Bible, because it contains the records of these events.

RADICAL VIEWS OF THE BIBLE.

While there are various and conflicting views of the Bible, there are two that, though widely apart, are equally destructive to the calm and thoughtful examination of its contents.

The first is called a "scientific criticism of the Scriptures." This destroys all belief in the Bible, either as the result of inspiration or as the work of man. The writers throughout are charged with deception and lying, and a work purporting to contain revelations from God is denounced as a tissue of falsehoods.

The other claims for the Bible, — not that it contains revelations from the Deity, — but that it is the actual "word of God;" that the men who wrote it were the mechanical instruments through whom God communicated with man; that the book is entire and complete, and as the word of God must be believed in its entirety without comment or distrust, notwithstanding its many mistakes and contradictions, its multiple pictures of the Deity, and its contrary and incongruous teachings.

While scientific criticism fosters *disbelief in the Bible,* the dogma of its verbal inspiration is a source of *disbelief in God,* and in religion as now generally taught.

SCIENTIFIC CRITICISM.

Of late years, critical investigations of the Bible by Ewald, Colenso, Kuenen, Hooykaas, and other scholars, have led to results startling in their character, and requiring careful consideration. These, with names more familiar, such as Dean Stanley, Matthew Arnold, Renan, Strauss, Neander, and many other writers, are referred to as authorities consulted, in a work called "The Bible of To-day, by John W. Chadwick, Minister of the Second Unitarian Church in Brooklyn, N. Y." This work claims to give "the principal results of the best historical and scientific criticism of the separate books of the Bible. They are (says the author), almost without exception, those which have been reached by many scholars of unimpeachable orthodoxy."

In a study of the Bible, a work of this character, claiming to represent the latest results of scientific criticism by scholars of unimpeachable orthodoxy, cannot be passed by without notice and examination.

Mr. Chadwick says, "Here in America, so far as I can judge, the Mosaic authorship of the Pentateuch is commonly assumed in all the Evangelical churches. A history purporting to begin with the beginning of the world, 4004 B.C., and to end in 1451 B.C., shortly after the death of Moses, whose death it piously records. All this is supposed to have been written by the hand of Moses, and to be a faithful and consistent account of things which really happened, and words which were really spoken by the persons or the deity to whom they are ascribed. If it were so, we should still have a history written at a distance, in many instances, of from five to five-and-twenty hundred years from the events recorded. To such a history, a theory of supernatural inspiration is absolutely necessary, if it is going to have any authority whatever. But the theory of supernatural inspiration, as well as the theory of Mosaic authorship, was never started till ten or a dozen centuries after the death of Moses. The theory of Mosaic authorship was part of a general system which, just before the beginning of the Christian era, ascribed the Old Testament books to those persons who figured in them most conspicuously; for example, the book of Joshua to Joshua, the books of Samuel to Samuel. But this conclusion of the Talmudists, ever the most uncritical of men, was without any critical justification whatever. There is not a sign that the book of Joshua was written by Joshua, or the books of Samuel by Samuel, or the five books of the Pentateuch by Moses." "So far was the composition of the Pentateuch from being contemporaneous with even the latest events which it narrates, that the oldest fragment of any size which it contains dates from the ninth century B.C. . . . The gap between this fragment and the patriarchal times is about a thousand years. This fragment, which the critics have agreed to call the Book of Covenants, extends from Exodus xxi. to xxiii. 19. The next considerable portion of the Pentateuch was probably written about B.C. 750, a dozen centuries and more from the events to which it gives most attention. These are the events of patriarchal times. In this document appear the patriarchal stories in their most charming form. . . . The Book of Covenants is included in this document, and also (according to some critics) another very considerable one is amalgamated with it, the author of which is sometimes called *the older Elohist*, because he uses the word Elohim for God. . . . Here, then, we have already three considerable documents included in the Pentateuch, but as yet it had not attained to half its present bulk. The next great addition was made in the time of King Josiah. This was the book of Deuteronomy. It was made public in 621 B.C., and had been written just before, six hundred and fifty years after the death of Moses. Soon after, it was incorporated with those parts of the Pentateuch which had been previously written."

This book is "much more of a manufacture than any previous portion of the Pentateuch. Here calculation takes the place of spontaneity. . . . The Deuteronomist went about deliberately to *invent* a great historic *fiction*. He knew what he wanted; namely, to abolish all idolatrous worship of Yahweh (Jehovah), all worship of all other gods, and, as a means to these ends, to confine the worship of Yahweh (Jehovah) to Jerusalem. . . . Choosing Moses as his mouthpiece, he represents him as calling the people together in the fortieth year of their wanderings in the wilderness, to refresh their memory of the Law which had been previously revealed to them, sternly commanding them to serve no other god but Yahweh (Jehovah)."

"The Deuteronomist does not by any means confine himself to the outward forms and ceremonies of religion. His book abounds in precepts which are political and civil and domestic in their character, and many of these are very noteworthy for their moral excellence. A spirit of equity and clemency in some of his social regulations allies them to the teachings of Jesus more closely than any other portion of the Pentateuch."

"And still the Pentateuch awaited an immense accession to its priestly elements, an immense addition to its bulk." This was the "Book of Origins," which Ewald says "dates from the time of Solomon."

THE BOOK OF ORIGINS. 109

This theory is not satisfactory to our author, who instead accepts the theory of Kuenen, that the Book of Origins dates from the fifth century B.C. "This Book of Origins," he says, "as it now exists, begins with the first line of Genesis, and runs in and out through all the other documents, not meddling much with Deuteronomy, up to the end of Joshua. It contains the first account of the creation and Adam's family register, an account of the Flood and Noah's family register. It deals with the Patriarchs much more summarily than do the earlier documents. In fact, until the time of Moses the portions of this book are only introductory to the writer's special theme, which is the publication of the Levitical Law. The book of Leviticus is almost entirely his, and the larger part of Numbers. Here, in with parts of Exodus, we have a sacerdotal code, which marks an immense advance in priestly notions and pretensions on the book of Deuteronomy. Whenever it is necessary to his purpose, the writer freely recasts the history of the Mosaic and pre-Mosaic times." This "Book of Origins, already incorporated with the remainder of the Pentateuch, . . . was promulgated by Ezra and Nehemiah, at Jerusalem, 445 B.C. Who had done this work of incorporation we do not know; . . . not Jerusalem, but Babylon, it is most likely, was the scene of this development. Not Sinai and the wilderness, but Babylon and Jerusalem, witnessed the promulgation of the Levitical Law. Its priest was Ezra, and not Aaron."

"We have here a book (the Pentateuch) made up of fragments arbitrarily forced together, which fragments made their appearance all the way along from 900 to 450 B.C. . . . There was a great stock of oral traditions to draw upon, and also various books, the names of which, in a few cases, have been preserved to us, as, for example, the book of Jasher, and the book of the Wars of Jehovah. But even the earliest of these was antedated a long time by the events recorded, and they are only quoted in the most fragmentary manner."

Of the book of Joshua he says, "We have reason to believe that the same hands that shaped the principal documents of the Pentateuch shaped the two principal fragments of the book of Joshua. These are, first, chapters i. to xiii.; second, chapters xiv. to xxiv. The book is naturally divided into these two sections. The first recites the story of Joshua's conquest of Canaan; the second, his division of the land among the tribes. The first is mainly from the Deuteronomist, the second is mainly by the 'author of the Book of Origins;' and the date of the book would be, say, 'by the Deuteronomist about 600 B.C., and by the author of Origins, after the captivity, about 450 B.C.'"

"In a book written so long after the events which it records, . . . we should not expect to find accurate history. But it may be said that in our day the best histories are the latest; for example, Green's History of the English People, and Freeman's History of the

THE DEUTERONOMIST. 111

Norman Conquest. True enough, but the superior value of these histories is based upon their critical use of contemporary documents. But the authors of Joshua had, in the first place, no contemporary documents that came within centuries of the events. . . . They were not in search of truth, their writings were tendency writings: that is, they were written to carry a point." The Deuteronomist "wanted the sanction of antiquity for his passionate exclusiveness, and for his centralized worship at Jerusalem." The author of Origins "wanted the sanction of antiquity for his Levitical enthusiasm."

"Judges is a wonderful treasury of almost contemporary traditions of the period between the conquest and the time of David, from about 1280 to 1050 B.C. or thereabout. According to Joshua, the tribes acted in perfect unity, subjugated Canaan entirely in one year, and divided its territory among the tribes. As there was never any such conquest as that of Joshua, recorded in the first of the thirteenth chapters, so was there never any such division of the territory as that of Joshua, recorded in the fourteenth to the twenty-seventh chapters."

"Judges is a tendency writing. It has a thesis to maintain, viz., that faithfulness to Jehovah is the only means of national prosperity; and was edited by one of the Prophets. The traditions embedded in his argument sufficiently confute his darling theories. His time was certainly no earlier than the seventh century B.C."

Ruth is also claimed as a "tendency writing, and dates about 400 B.C."

Of the first and second books of Samuel our author says, "It is not likely that these books attained their present form till just before or soon after the beginning of the captivity. The object of the writer was to glorify Samuel and David at the expense of Saul. . . . The writer made use of various legends, written and oral, and joined them together in a very crude and blundering fashion."

Next, "we have the two books of Kings. The books are written with a purpose, to show that only in the faithful service of Jehovah is there safety and success for kings and people. The suffering of Israel and Judah are the merited punishments of their idolatry and disobedience. Probably the work was finished about 562 B.C., and was written in Babylon, by one who was a captive there. . . . He made use of many written sources," and "sometimes stands corrected by the narratives which he incorporates into his own. But, with the exception of the incidental history embodied in the Prophets, he is our only historian of Israel, for five hundred years, who is at all trustworthy. With the books of Kings ended the treatment of history from a prophetic standpoint."

"The books of Chronicles go over the same ground, but they pervert our knowledge more than they increase it." They "were written about 300 B.C., and are a reconstruction of the entire history of Israel, in order to compel the sanction of that history for that scheme of priestly worship which had been developed in Babylon and set up in Jerusalem by Ezra and Nehemiah. . . . Whatever his materials, they were all fluid in the heat of his Levitic zeal, and all received the impress of his cherished theory, that the acceptable worship of Jehovah consisted in the minute observance of a ceremonial and sacrificial system of religion centralized in the one temple at Jerusalem. . . . The persistent idolatry of the nation is scarcely mentioned, except when it is needed as a background to bring out the virtue of the kings who labored to suppress it. . . . David and Solomon are idealized; the credit of designing the temple and the organization of the temple service is given to David. . . . Nothing remains for Solomon but to carry out the plans of David. . . . The fondness of Solomon for other forms of worship is passed over lightly, or his wives are charged with causing his defection." . . . "Manasseh, whose reign lasted the longest of any king of Judah, and the most prosperous and peaceful, offered a very knotty problem to the Chronicler, who, with Ezekiel, believes that national prosperity depended on the faithful service of Jehovah, for Manasseh fostered all the abominations of the Canaanites . . . and so Manasseh is made to suffer captivity, and to repent in dust and ashes for his wickedness, . . . but for neither repentance nor captivity is there any warrant in the earlier and more truthful histories. This story is, perhaps, the earliest prototype of a numerous class of famous recantations, of which Voltaire's and Thomas Paine's are modern illustrations, and equally without a particle of evidence." [1]

Of the other books of the Old Testament, our author writes in much the same manner. They were books written to serve a purpose. Of the predictions contained in the prophetical books (he says), "some of the more general were fulfilled, the most were doomed to utter disappointment." [2]

He sums up the political history of the Hebrews

---

[1] Relative to this statement of our author regarding Manasseh, among the Assyrian archives, as translated by George Smith, Esq., of the British Museum, is the following. About 680 B.C., Esarhaddon, king of Assyria, " marched against Sidon, which he besieged, captured, and destroyed." At this time the whole of Palestine and the surrounding places submitted to Esarhaddon, who gives a list of the kings, and among them is Manasseh, king of Judah. Some years after, he made an expedition against Judah; a portion of the record is defaced, but this statement remains, "Manasseh, king of Judah, submitted to Esarhaddon;" "he carried large numbers of Israelites away captive, and replaced them by colonies of Babylonians, and he bound Manasseh, king of Judah, and brought him to Babylon." There is no record of his return, which is stated in the Bible to have been the fact. Rev. A. H. Sayce, the editor of " Smith's History of Babylonia," in a footnote, says, " It was while Esarhaddon was holding his court at Babylon, that Manasseh of Judah was brought there captive. . . . The character and rule of Esarhaddon seem to have been mild, and the release of Manasseh from captivity is paralleled by other similar acts of clemency on his part."

[2] In a previous chapter we have carefully examined the prophecies against Egypt, Assyria, and Babylon, and have obtained from Babylonian and Assyrian cylinders, as translated by Professors Smith, Sayce, and others, and from ancient and modern history, facts showing their complete fulfilment, or that they are still active and in process of being fulfilled.

as follows: "In all strictness this does not begin until the exodus from Egypt in 1320 B.C., and there are some things antecedent to the exodus which we can dimly fashion. For centuries before the exodus — such would appear to be the import of the patriarchal stories — Semitic hordes from beyond the Euphrates were pushing down into Arabia, Palestine, and Egypt. Sometimes the races already in possession forced them back. The journey of Abraham was most likely the emigration of a tribe; its starting-point, Ur of the Chaldees, being about one hundred and fifty miles due south of modern Erzerum, on the south side of the Taurus.[1] The journey of Jacob back into Haran was a great backward movement of the swaying mass. His subsequent return to Canaan, another great migration."

"Joseph in Egypt possibly represents the first wave of migration into Egypt, followed ere long by that of kindred tribes, but these Hebrews were not the first Semitic tribes to go down, they were the last. About 2100 B.C., Lower Egypt was conquered by a Semitic race, which ruled over it till 1580 B.C., when

[1] Recent explorations show that our author is probably mistaken as to the situation of "Ur" of the Chaldees, which was a large and important city at the time of Abram, the capital of Southern Babylonia, now "represented by the mounds of 'Mugheir,' about six miles from the Euphrates, on its western bank, about latitude 31°. It was probably not far from the old mouth of the Euphrates." "The city of Ur was devoted to the worship of the moon god, called in early times Ur, and the place itself appears to have been named, after that divinity, the city of Ur."

it was driven out by the native Egyptians, who had maintained themselves in Upper Egypt. The Hebrews were a later wave of immigration, and they remained in Egypt after the shepherd kings (of whom Joseph's Pharaoh was one) had gone. . . . A king arose who knew not Joseph. In other words, the native Egyptians had reconquered Lower Egypt. So long as the Israelites could be kept contented, they made a living wall between the banished Hyksos and the Egyptians. But they at last grew restless under the oppression of the great Rameses II., and under his son Menephta (Amenophis) they rebelled, and, aided by the Hyksos, they broke away from their allegiance, and resumed their old nomadic life. Such was the exodus, the Bible date of which is 1491. Instead of this date, write 1320 B.C., as the best approximation we can make by carefully comparing the Pentateuch and Manetho (an Egyptian historian) and the monuments."

"The towering personality of Moses was equal to the task of holding them together in the act of their rebellion and deliverance, but after that there was little united action. The different tribes went each its way to plant and graze. . . . Some of them conquered the district east of the Jordan, with the help of the Moabites. Others, under Joshua, with the help of the Midianites and Edomites, pushed their way into Canaan about forty years after the exodus, and there they remained ignorant tribes, with little civilization or religion, among the more civilized nations around them."

"To Saul belongs the glory of arousing the sentiment of nationality and fusing the discordant tribal elements into a political unit. His reign was short, but did him no dishonor."

David was a fierce soldier. "He had none of Saul's scruples about slaughtering the Canaanites. He was every inch a king, and consolidated the nation. He subdued its enemies, and utilized the zeal alike of priests and prophets."

It is hardly necessary for us to follow this author any further. The extracts from his book which we have given reveal the character and animus of the work, and they show his utter disbelief in the Bible either as a historical or religious book.

Now let us see what this writer claims.

All the books forming the Pentateuch were manufactured.

The oldest portion of the Old Testament, the "Book of Covenants," was written about the ninth century before Christ.

The patriarchal stories, about B.C. 750.

The book of Deuteronomy, "a deliberate invention," "a great historic fiction," was written in the time of King Josiah, and made public B.C. 621.

The "Book of Origins," "containing what is now scattered through Genesis, Exodus, the greater part of Numbers and Leviticus, was written about B.C. 450, by some one unknown, to give the sanction of antiquity to the Levitical laws, and was promulgated by Ezra and Nehemiah."

118 ORIGIN OF HEBREW SCRIPTURES.

"The same hands wrote the history of the division of the land, fourteenth to twenty-fourth chapters of Joshua."

"The history of the conquest in the first thirteen chapters was written by the Deuteronomist." "Both of these authors wrote for a purpose, and each falsified history to carry out his object."

The author of Judges has a thesis to maintain, and "it was written for a purpose by one of the prophets."

Ruth, the same.

The books of Samuel are also false, and were written for an object during the captivity in Babylon.

The books of the Kings, the same.

The books of Chronicles, worse than all. They were written about B.C. 300. "The materials of the author were all fluid in the heat of his Levitical zeal, and all received the impress of his cherished theory."

All these books, our author says, are false, written by men who, impelled by the desire to advance their own views, falsified the truths of history and the events of their own time, and manufactured these various books, skilfully interweaving a few old tales and traditions.

According to this writer, Abraham, Isaac, and Jacob are myths; their stories, specimens of the novelist's art; or, if they ever existed, they were names of nomadic migratory hordes. The slavery of the Israelites is a fiction. The contest between Jehovah and the Egyptian gods, a myth. In fact, there was no Jehovah, except as created by the novelist who composed the story. There was no river of blood, no frogs, flies, or locusts; no murrain on cattle; no boils; no hail and fire; no darkness, nor death of the first-born; no passing over of the angel of death; no passover instituted until long years afterward; no crossing of the Red Sea nor destruction of Pharaoh's hosts; no Sinai, no earthquakes, clouds, or trumpets; no delivery of the law; no covenant; no worship; no pillar of cloud and fire; no forty years in the wilderness; no conquest of Canaan. These are all merely the dramatic characters and incidents of the fiction.

There were no prophets except those who prophesy in general terms; or, where the predictions were specific and particular, they were never fulfilled.

In fact, according to Mr. Chadwick, the Hebrew Scriptures are a tissue of falsehoods from beginning to end, and every writer thereof a deliberate falsifier.

. . . .

In the Pentateuch we have the only account in the world of a revelation made to and a contract or covenant made with man by the Deity until the time of Christ. In these books, we trace the incipient steps in the revelation to and covenants made with Abraham, Isaac, and Jacob; then the greater revelation and covenant made through Moses with the Hebrews. With these revelations is the promise that the seed of Abraham shall become a great nation, and shall inherit the land pointed out to him. This promise is fulfilled by their servitude to the Egyptians. Their delivery from bondage by means of miracles of a nature before unknown; their departure from Egypt; the many and unexampled miracles of the journey; the delivery of the law; the covenant with Jehovah; the forty years' instruction; the final entrance into, the conquering, and the taking possession of this land; all these things are accomplished with the aid of Jehovah, by ways perfectly adapted to the end desired, and thoroughly unique in the means taken to that end. Yet we are asked to believe that there is not a particle of truth in these statements, that several hundred years after the events described are said to have taken place, some unknown writers of the Hebrews, with imaginations greater far than any that have appeared before or since, and writing at periods from two hundred and fifty to five hundred years apart, and from four hundred to one thousand years after the events related, created this whole story. The allegories of Genesis; the stories of the patriarchs' lives; their communion with God; the promises made to them; their various adventures until their descendants are brought into Egypt, and there increase to a great nation; the life and character of Moses, and the unique miracles, both in Egypt and Sinai, are the work of these writers. They also created the being and character of Jehovah, no such god having been found in the records of any other nation. Without correspondence or unity of interest, they unitedly carry this nation, the creature of their separate brains, through all these strange vicissitudes, (experiences entirely unknown to any other nation or people), and bring it by these unexampled means to its haven of rest.

These fictions, we are told, were discovered and adopted by Ezra and Nehemiah, and by them were applied and fitted on to the then existing Hebrew nation; such previous traditions and writings as they had being of course altered to agree with it; thus giving us a book thoroughly homogeneous in its character, similar ideas of Jehovah being presented by all its various writers; the teachings of Moses continually referred to as if true; the covenant with Jehovah repeatedly re-adopted, and the fiction established by frequent references to the incidents of their invented history. And this fabrication is so natural as to have imposed upon the Jews of a later time, who, even unto this day, believe in its truth. It was also believed in by Christ and his apostles, and by Christians until now. What miracles are these, greater far than any mentioned in the Bible, or ever before heard of in history or fiction!

We are asked to believe that all the books of the Hebrew scriptures are figments of the imagination, written by prophet, priest, and scribe, for the purpose of each carrying out his own plans and ideas, yet all agreeing in the delineation of the great characters and events of their nation, which were, notwithstanding, entirely fictitious. Can such a thing be possible? Yet this is the ground taken by this writer, this is the result of his statements. Can we believe this? Is it not more impossible than the wildest tale of Munchausen? Does it not require more credulity than "The Thousand and One Tales"?

Here is a writer who freely charges the Old Testament authors with tendency writing, with falsifying the truths of history and the events of their own times, with inventing stories and incidents with the novelist's art, all to serve and carry out their own private views and purposes.

Can there be a more thorough specimen of such tendency writing than the book we have been examining, as shown in its vain endeavor to dethrone Jehovah, in its ability to stumble over and not see the hundreds of miracles that obstruct its path, and in its blind denial of the fulfilment of prophecy?

Any one would suppose that the certainty with which the author makes his statements, and announces the dates at which the several books were written, was the result of combined scientific examination and criticism; but what do we find? Let us compare the results arrived at by Mr. Chadwick and several of the prominent German critics regarding the Pentateuch.

BOOK OF COVENANTS.

CHADWICK.	EWALD.	COLENSO.	KUENEN.
B.C. 900.	B.C. 1095.	Myth.	B.C. 1320.
B.C. 750.			

BOOK OF ORIGINS.

CHADWICK.	EWALD.	COLENSO.	KUENEN.
B.C. 445.	B.C. 1075.	B.C. 1095.	B.C. 800.
			B.C. 445.
	DEUTERONOMY.		
B.C. 621.	B.C. 621.	Legendary.	B.C. 621.

This is the result of *Scientific Criticism.* What a wonderful *science!*

VERBAL INSPIRATION.

The second radical view of the Bible is that of verbal inspiration. According to Kitto's "Encyclopædia of Biblical Literature," an accepted exponent of Trinitarian beliefs, the dogma of the inspiration of the Scriptures rests upon the assertion that "the books of which it is composed are of divine authority; that they are entire, incorrupt, complete," and that "this divine authorship can be proved."

In attempting to sustain this assertion, while acknowledging that doubts have arisen respecting the authorship of the Pentateuch, — several Trinitarian authorities having stated that its author is unknown, — Kitto finally, as the result of his study, ascribes it to Moses.

He also considers it "highly probable that the whole book of Joshua, up to the twenty-eighth verse of the last chapter, was composed by Joshua." Later Trinitarian authority pronounces the author of Joshua unknown.

Kitto says the author of Judges is unknown. Ruth also unknown. First and second books of Samuel unknown, but thinks they were written by Samuel, Nathan, and Gad. First and second books of Kings is a compilation, the author unknown, but Jewish tradition makes Jeremiah the author. First and second books of Chronicles unknown, but are ascribed to Ezra and finished by Daniel. Book of Job unknown. Psalms of David unknown; a portion were completed during the reign of Hezekiah, others in the reign of Manasseh, Nehemiah, and even to the date of the Maccabees. Ecclesiastes unknown. The remaining books of the Hebrew Scriptures are generally ascribed to the persons whose name they bear, but without authority or proof.

The Bible date of Malachi is about 400 B.C. The intervening period to the time of the Christ is partially covered by apocryphal books, bringing the biblical history down to about B.C. 160.

Thus we find, by Trinitarian authority, that there is a great uncertainty regarding the authorship of the principal books comprising the Old Testament.

THE CHRONOLOGY OF THE HEBREW SCRIPTURES

is so generally acknowledged to be unreliable that it is hardly necessary to more than mention the fact that between Usher's (the Bible chronology) and the Septuagint there is a difference of 1504 years.

THE CANON OF SCRIPTURE.

Kitto defines the Canon to be "the authoritative standard of religion and morals, composed of those writings which have been given for this purpose by God to men." He says, in order to establish the canon of Scripture it is necessary to show, —

First, "that all the books of which it is composed are of divine authority."

Second, "that they are entire and incorrupt."

Third, "that, having them, it is complete without any addition from any other source;" and

Fourth, "that it comprises the whole of those books for which divine authority can be proved."

"It is obvious," he says, "that if any of these four particulars be not true, Scripture cannot be the sole and supreme standard of religious truth and duty."

In support of the first of the above requirements, "we want to know," he says,

First, "that these books were really written by the persons whose names they bear."

Second, "we want to be satisfied that these persons were commonly reputed and held by their contemporaries to be assisted by the Divine Spirit in what they wrote."

Third, "we want to be sure that care was taken by those to whom their writings were first addressed, that they should be preserved entire and incorrupt;" and

Fourth, "we want to see . . . that their authors really assumed to be under the Divine direction in what they wrote."

With these requirements before us, let us see the

result of our examination of the Hebrew scriptures. In support of these positions, as applied to the Pentateuch, Kitto quotes Deut. xxxi. 9, 26, to which we have added the twenty-fourth and twenty-fifth verses. "And Moses wrote this law, and delivered it unto the priests, the sons of Levi, which bare the ark of the covenant of the Lord, and unto all the elders of Israel. . . . And it came to pass, when Moses had made an end of writing the words of this law in a book until they were finished, that Moses commanded the Levites, which bare the ark of the covenant of the Lord, saying, Take this book of the law and put it in the side of the ark of the covenant of the Lord your God, that it may be there for a witness against thee."

It is evident that Genesis, one of the five books of the Pentateuch, is no part of the "Book of the Law." *That* probably consisted of the laws now contained in Exodus, Leviticus, Numbers, with the law and the covenant, and its record of blessings and cursings recorded by Moses in Deuteronomy, together with the renewed covenant made through Joshua with the Israelites, as recorded in the twenty-fourth chapter of Joshua, which was added thereto.

As applied to Joshua, Kitto quotes Josh. xxiv. 26, "And Joshua wrote the words in the book of the law of God."

The context here shows that this writing referred to the covenant with Jehovah, which the Hebrews had at this time renewed.

THE BOOK OF THE LAW. 127

Kitto declares the authors of Judges, Ruth, Job, and Ecclesiastes unknown.

Of the first and second books of Samuel, first and second books of Kings, first and second books of Chronicles, the authors are unknown. The authorship of many of the later books of the Hebrew scriptures is disputed, but they are of less consequence than those mentioned.

On applying these tests we find not one of the ancient books of the Hebrew scriptures, outside of the prophetical writings, can sustain them, except portions of Exodus, Leviticus, Numbers, and Deuteronomy. Kitto claims it for the Pentateuch and Joshua, but, as is shown, with only partial effect, and other Trinitarian writers pronounce the authors of Genesis and Joshua "unknown."

There is *no proof* that

First, "all the books of which it (the Old Testament) is composed were written by divine authority."

Second, "that they are entire and incorrupt."

Third, "that it (the Canon) is complete without any addition."

Fourth, "that divine authority can be proved for any of these books."

There is no proof

First, "that they were really written by the persons whose names they bear."

Second, that the authors "were assisted by the Divine Spirit."

Third, "that the books were preserved entire and uncorrupt;" or

Fourth, that "their authors assumed to be under Divine direction in what they wrote."

Moses was ordered to put down certain things in a book, and the prophets alone in the Hebrew scriptures claim to speak by divine authority and to have been divinely inspired.

Thus we find the authorship of most of the ancient books forming the Hebrew scriptures doubtful or unknown, its chronology generally rejected, and the claim of verbal inspiration unsupported, and in fact disproved, by the very requirements laid down for its establishment, consequently the portion of the Bible known as the Old Testament cannot be "the authoritative standard of religion and morals" that it has been claimed to be. It cannot "be the sole and supreme standard of religious truth and duty." In fact, in the teachings of Moses, it inculcates but a very low standard of religion or morals.

It certainly is not the word of God, nor was it written by inspiration of God, yet it contains inspired utterances, and records acts and deeds also inspired. Its statements are undoubtedly founded on fact and mainly correct. In the coincidence of ideas, it bears evidence of the authenticity of its sources and the honesty of its purpose. Above all, it contains the records of revelations made by the Deity to man, and of covenants made by God with man; and these revelations give to it a character and value possessed by no other book except the Christian scriptures.

The Bible itself makes no claim to verbal or other

inspiration; the prophets speak by the inspiration of Jehovah; Moses refers his power to Jehovah, and claims to have received communications from him.

The only claim made by the book itself is in its titles, the "Old Testament," the "New Testament." Testament means the will or purpose of the Deity as shown in the Old Covenant and in the New Covenant. A covenant, or contract, is a mutual agreement made between two or more parties.

The old covenant, under which the Hebrews acted, was made between Jehovah, on the one side, and the Hebrew people, acting through Moses as their agent, on the other.

The people, on their part, agreed to honor and serve Jehovah as their God, and to worship no other god; they bound themselves and their children to the faithful performance of these obligations under penalties of the curses of the covenant.

"Behold, I set before you this day a blessing and a curse: a blessing if ye obey the commandments of the Lord your God, which I command you this day; and a curse if ye will not obey the commandments of the Lord your God, but turn aside out of the way which I command you this day, to go after other gods which ye have not known."

The agreement on the part of Jehovah was that he would be the tutelary or national God of the Hebrews; he would advance their interests, and bless them with the blessings of the covenant as long as they continued faithfully to worship and serve him. If they failed in their allegiance to him, he would punish them by sending on them the curses of the same covenant. This covenant was sealed with all due formalities by the contracting parties. It was a contract with the Hebrews, a people distinct and separate from all other people, and binding on them alone. It was made with them as against all nations then existing, and it was repeatedly renewed and indorsed by the Hebrews, thus evidencing the truth of the original records, and witnessing to the binding force of the covenant.

This covenant is entirely earthly; its blessings are earthly peace, happiness, riches, health, plenty, and prosperity, and its curses are also earthly trouble, poverty, sickness, famine, adversity, war, and captivity.

If we read the Hebrew scriptures in this light, we shall find the constant and exact fulfilment of the promises and threats of the covenant.

Christians have erred in placing the Hebrew scriptures on a plane of equality with the Christian scriptures. The coming of Christ and the promulgation of the new covenant open to all mankind, closed and ended the old and partial covenant made with one nation. Christ says, "The law and the prophets *were until John,* since that time the kingdom of God is preached."

The covenant of the law ceased with the advent of the Christ, and the requirements of the Jewish religion actually ended in the downfall of the Jewish nation. All its forms, ceremonies, and sacrificial system are gone; it was a system established in an early period of the world's history, with an ignorant nation, and suited to their capabilities and knowledge; it was established to introduce to and keep alive in the world a knowledge of God, and that purpose was accomplished.

The Jews cannot now fulfil its requirements: the Jehovah of the Jews is no more; he has gone forever, has ceased to exist, and God, our heavenly Father, is all in all.

The principal value of the Old Testament to the Christian, other than its literary character, its beautiful religious imagery, and its many noble utterances, is that therein we have a record of the first revelations from God, and the first contracts entered into between God and man. Here we have the incipient steps towards the revelation of that great evangel which commenced in Abram and continued in Moses and the prophets, culminated in Jesus the Christ, which gives to the Bible pre-eminence over all scriptures of all times and all nations.

The Bible is the only book which claims to contain a revelation direct from the Deity. In this the Bible is unique, and in this only can a claim be made, not of verbal inspiration, but of divine revelation. All others contain the religious utterances of men only, some evidently from divine sources, the origin of which are now unknown, notably the Hindu and Persian ancient religious writings or scriptures, which are full of faith and trust in God, in his love and care, and in immortality; and they teach purity of thought and life.

The revelation to and covenant with Abram was personal, not national. It was crude, initiatory, requiring faith and obedience to the light given him, and was accepted by him in the rite of circumcision. The larger revelation made through Moses to the Hebrews was national, made to that people alone. It was also accompanied by a covenant which was accepted and ratified by that nation, and was on many occasions renewed. It has not, nor ever had, the slightest claim on any other people, nation, or tongue.

The final and full revelation made through Jesus the Christ to all mankind is also accompanied by a covenant already signed on the part of God, which is open to all of every tongue and nation for their acceptance or rejection.

BRIGHT AND BREEZY BOOKS OF TRAVEL
— — BY SIX BRIGHT WOMEN — — —

A WINTER IN CENTRAL AMERICA AND MEXICO
By HELEN J. SANBORN. Cloth, $1.50.
"A bright, attractive narrative by a wide-awake Boston girl."

A SUMMER IN THE AZORES, with a Glimpse of Madeira
By Miss C. ALICE BAKER. Little Classic style. Cloth, gilt edges, $1.25.
"Miss Baker gives us a breezy, entertaining description of these picturesque islands. She is an observing traveller, and makes a graphic picture of the quaint people and customs." — *Chicago Advance.*

LIFE AT PUGET SOUND
With sketches of travel in Washington Territory, British Columbia, Oregon, and California. By CAROLINE C. LEIGHTON. 16mo, cloth, $1.50.
"Your chapters on Puget Sound have charmed me. Full of life, deeply interesting, and with just that class of facts, and suggestions of truth, that cannot fail to help the Indian and the Chinese." — WENDELL PHILLIPS.

EUROPEAN BREEZES
By MARGERY DEANE. Cloth, gilt top, $1.50. Being chapters of travel through Germany, Austria, Hungary, and Switzerland, covering places not usually visited by Americans in making "the Grand Tour of the Continent," by the accomplished writer of "Newport Breezes."
"A very bright, fresh and amusing account, which tells us about a host of things we never heard of before, and is worth two ordinary books of European travel." — *Woman's Journal.*

BEATEN PATHS; or, A Woman's Vacation in Europe
By ELLA W. THOMPSON. 16mo, cloth. $1.50.
A lively and chatty book of travel, with pen-pictures humorous and graphic, that are decidedly out of the "beaten paths" of description.

AN AMERICAN GIRL ABROAD
By Miss ADELINE TRAFTON, author of "His Inheritance," "Katherine Earle," etc. 16mo. Illustrated. $1.50.
"A sparkling account of a European trip by a wide-awake, intelligent, and irrepressible American girl. Pictured with a freshness and vivacity that is delightful." — *Utica Observer.*

CURTIS GUILD'S TRAVELS

BRITONS AND MUSCOVITES; or, Traits of Two Empires
Cloth, $2.00.

OVER THE OCEAN; or, Sights and Scenes in Foreign Lands
By CURTIS GUILD, editor of "The Boston Commercial Bulletin.' Crown 8vo. Cloth, $2.50.
"The utmost that any European tourist can hope to do is to tell the old story in a somewhat fresh way, and Mr. Guild has succeeded in every part of his book in doing this." — *Philadelphia Bulletin.*

ABROAD AGAIN; or, Fresh Forays in Foreign Fields
Uniform with "Over the Ocean." By the same author Crown 8vo. Cloth, $2.50.
"He has given us a life-picture. Europe is done in a style that must serve as an invaluable guide to those who go 'over the ocean,' as well as an interesting companion." — *Halifax Citizen.*

Sold by all booksellers, and sent by mail, postpaid, on receipt of price
LEE AND SHEPARD Publishers Boston

NARRATIVES OF NOTED TRAVELLERS

GERMANY SEEN WITHOUT SPECTACLES; or, Random Sketches of Various Subjects, Penned from Different Standpoints in the Empire
By HENRY RUGGLES, late United States Consul at the Island of Malta, and at Barcelona, Spain. $1.50.
"Mr. Ruggles writes briskly: he chats and gossips, slashing right and left with stout American prejudices, and has made withal a most entertaining book." — *New-York Tribune.*

TRAVELS AND OBSERVATIONS IN THE ORIENT, with a Hasty Flight in the Countries of Europe
By WALTER HARRIMAN (ex-Governor of New Hampshire). $1.50.
"The author, in his graphic description of these sacred localities, refers with great aptness to scenes and personages which history has made famous. It is a chatty narrative of travel." — *Concord Monitor.*

FORE AND AFT
A Story of Actual Sea-Life. By ROBERT B. DIXON, M.D. $1.25.
Travels in Mexico, with vivid descriptions of manners and customs, form a large part of this striking narrative of a fourteen-months' voyage.

VOYAGE OF THE PAPER CANOE
A Geographical Journey of Twenty-five Hundred Miles from Quebec to the Gulf of Mexico. By NATHANIEL H. BISHOP. With numerous illustrations and maps specially prepared for this work. Crown 8vo. $1.50.
"Mr. Bishop did a very bold thing, and has described it with a happy mixture of spirit, keen observation, and *bonhomie.*" — *London Graphic.*

FOUR MONTHS IN A SNEAK-BOX
A Boat Voyage of Twenty-six Hundred Miles down the Ohio and Mississippi Rivers, and along the Gulf of Mexico. By NATHANIEL H. BISHOP. With numerous maps and illustrations. $1.50.
"His glowing pen-pictures of 'shanty-boat' life on the great rivers are true to life. His descriptions of persons and places are graphic." — *Zion's Herald.*

A THOUSAND MILES' WALK ACROSS SOUTH AMERICA, Over the Pampas and the Andes
By NATHANIEL H. BISHOP. Crown 8vo. New edition. Illustrated. $1.50.
"Mr. Bishop made this journey when a boy of sixteen, has never forgotten it, and tells it in such a way that the reader will always remember it, and wish there had been more."

CAMPS IN THE CARIBBEES
Being the Adventures of a Naturalist Bird-hunting in the West-India Islands. By FRED A. OBER. New edition. With maps and illustrations. $1.50.
"During two years he visited mountains, forests, and people, that few, if any, tourists had ever reached before. He carried his camera with him, and photographed from nature the scenes by which the book is illustrated." — *Louisville Courier-Journal.*

ENGLAND FROM A BACK WINDOW; With Views of Scotland and Ireland
By J. M. BAILEY, the "'Danbury News' Man." 12mo. $1.00.
"The peculiar humor of this writer is well known. The British Isles have never before been looked at in just the same way, — at least, not by any one who has notified us of the fact. Mr. Bailey's travels possess, accordingly, a value of their own for the reader, no matter how many previous records of journeys in the mother country he may have read." — *Rochester Express.*

Sold by all booksellers, and sent by mail, postpaid, on receipt of price

LEE AND SHEPARD Publishers Boston

www.ingramcontent.com/pod-product-compliance
Lightning Source LLC
Chambersburg PA
CBHW022135160426
43197CB00009B/1295